MW00425789

made sense. As we age, we usually retire from the workforce, losing a core friend group. Health issues often restrict a person from getting out in social settings. For many in previous generations, it was more natural for the elderly to be the loneliest demographic.

But now, the healthiest and most active social group is the loneliest?

We should be very alarmed at this new trend.

Suicidality, substance abuse, addictions of all types, depression, and out-of-control weight gain are all on the rise since the lockdowns. People who are isolated do harmful things.

Historically, isolated people are easily drawn into a *mass delusion*. Loneliness and a lack of connection with others is understood to be the most critical factor in large numbers of people doing horrific things to one another in a desperate and sad attempt to connect with a "virtuous" group.

2. *Lack of Meaning Making*

People who are isolated and lonely by nature come to see life as lacking meaning. Working from home and not being involved in the lives of others naturally produces a sense of futility—of not making a difference in the world. Not being embedded in a strong social network, as is typical of an office or other work setting, leads one to sense that what they do doesn't make a difference.

This lack of meaning is becoming stronger over time. With the increasing technological nature of life, less importance is placed on *people interacting*, and more is done *virtually through a device*. *Efficiency* and *profit* have become more important than *contact, grace,* and *kindness*. Smart devices are making humans *seem* less needed—although this too is a delusion.

Our ever-electronically-connected state has only *increased the likelihood and strength of the conditions needed for a mass atrocity under the conditions of mass delusion.*

3. *Free-floating Anxiety*

Even before the COVID debacle, anxiety was on a significant upswing, especially among young adults.[6] Free-floating anxiety is not something related to a specific threat that a person perceives they have control over; rather, it is a vague sense of fear and even panic about something threatening that is out of one's control. People experiencing this anxiety feel helpless, which is very important when it comes to mass delusion.

Anxiety and depression used to be more common for people in their forties. Now it is rampant for people in their twenties. Antidepressants and psychotropic drugs are being prescribed at record levels; the people of the western world are coming completely unhinged.

Anxious people naturally seek relief from their discomfort. They are prime targets for delusion.

4. *Free-floating Aggression and Frustration*

This naturally follows from the first three conditions.

An isolated person desperately needing purpose, control, connection, and calming, yet seemingly unable to achieve it, becomes aggressively angry and frustrated. And this need for aggression is directed at no one in particular.

Quite naturally, people in this agitated state begin looking for an object to attach their anger to. Such people become extremely willing to participate in a cause that is identified to them as *the problem*.

For the Soviets, it was the wealthy.

For the Germans, it was the actions and the "scientific" pseudo-inferiority of the Jews.

Embracing the pathetic reasonings of the ideologues who promoted these solutions gave the isolated people a feeling of connection. They were united in a common cause to address the

CHAPTER 2

Perfect Fear Casts Out Love

To him who is in fear everything rustles.
—Sophocles

There are very few monsters who warrant the fear we have of them.
—Andre Gide

For you did not receive the spirit of slavery to fall back into fear, but you have received the Spirit of adoption as sons, by whom we cry, Abba! Father!
—Yeshua of Nazareth

There is no fear in love, but perfect love casts out fear. For fear has to do with punishment, and whoever fears has not been perfected in love.
—John the apostle

"I do not associate with the unvaccinated!" my flight surgeon said sternly, pointing me into the farthest corner of the small exam room we shared.

I had just stood up to hand him some required medical paperwork. I continued forward, calmly handed him the stack of paper, and gently said, "There you go."

What had evoked this doctor's anger was my answer to a question he had asked, but understand that *this* doctor is an old military buddy of mine who I care for deeply. Our relationship goes way back, and I wanted to preserve our friendship.

But prior to this somewhat heated declaration from him, he had asked me casually, "Which vaccine did you get?" This was in reference to the COVID-19 shots.

"None," I replied. "I've had COVID at least twice, maybe three times, and I had my antibodies tested again last week." I pulled out my phone to show him the results. "They are substantially elevated."

His jaw tightened. "Those won't do anything for you!"

I've learned to restrain my inner voice—usually. And fortunately, today was one of those days when a sarcastic reply was contained. I was instantly thinking that *true* vaccines have worked effectively by stimulating antibody protection—which of course is what the mRNA vaccines do *not* do. His statement about my antibodies not helping seemed rather strongly unmedical.

"I have the Moderna vaccine. I can give it to you while you are here today," he offered.

"No, I'm good," was my soft reply. He was getting more and more upset with me.

On the one hand, it seemed funny, but also it was sad.

He clearly was afraid of *me* in spite of the fact that I had natural immunity—while he had been fully vaccinated with one of the highly touted mRNA shots. *He* was fully vaccinated *and* fearful. *He* was *afraid* of me, angry with me, while I literally would have been more than willing to give him the usual bear hug I give to my former military comrades.

Could he not see that he was offering me, by giving the Moderna shot, uncertainty and fear? He may have claimed to believe that the vaccine he was offering gave protection, but his behavior clearly indicated that he knew it did not.

And back to our earlier discussion on mass delusion, can you see how quickly he changed his view of me from being his old friend to being in the identity group *unvaccinated*—someone he would not associate with? Even though he was supposedly fully protected, as he wanted me to be, his actions were those of someone delusional and therefore ignorantly cruel. His claim of my need to get the

Moderna or any other mRNA shot was self-refuting, as indicated by his behavior.

One thing is clear about the medical profession. They are people just like everyone else. I am very thankful for the doctors, nurses, researchers, and vaccine developers, yet they are not infallible, nor does their substantial education make them immune to group think or mass delusion psychosis. It is clear from watching many medical doctors during the course of the Wuhan virus that some adopted a position of pro-vaccine in spite of the fact that the mRNA shots did not meet the definition of a vaccine.[15] Further, the method of function of these shots substantially modifies your cell's God-designed immune response—and causes what is appearing to be a whole host of other serious side effects.[16] One 2021 study outlined numerous incipient pathways of harm to those who have received the mRNA shots, noting that "they harbor the possibility of potentially tragic and even catastrophic unforeseen consequences."[17] The evidence is still incomplete as of this writing, but there is indication that the mRNA shots may contribute to rapidly growing cancer.[18]

My old friend, a fully-vaccinated medical doctor, is treating an old friend like crap because of fear. He is a believer in our Lord as well, and as the quote from the apostle John specifies at the beginning of this chapter, there is no fear in God's perfect love.

Something is wrong with this fearful and angry man's faith.

The title of this chapter is an inversion of a scripture. I accidently misquoted John the apostle one Sunday morning while teaching class by saying, "Perfect fear casts out love." I knew something was amiss instantly due to the rampant snickering going on. One brother lovingly let me in on my verbal faux pas. "You said, 'Perfect fear casts out love.' You got it backward!"

I was shocked, realizing that I had totally misquoted what the Word actually said, and then someone else in the class spoke a word of grace. "But that is absolutely true!"

It truly is true. Perfect fear *does* cast out love. We have an epidemic of un-love in our society and even among believers. It is hate induced by irrational fear.

Fear frequently prevents us from seeing the full picture, something known as *perceptual narrowing.*

The way my doctor-friend treated me was hateful, and it hurt. I realized that this would likely be my last-ever office visit with him, because he, in his fully vaccinated fear, does not associate with old friends who choose to rely on the loving care and designed immunity that God provides. He was also mocking the truth I had been taught by God of living only in fear of God himself.

Self-Check

Can I be your Dave? If you have a lot of fear present in your life, you have a serious spiritual issue.

Use your Creator-bestowed imagination. See yourself at the Sermon on the Mount as recorded in the letter of Matthew, and note that at a certain point in his talk, Jesus starts a particular point by saying, "Do not …"

When the King of us all says, "Do not," don't you think we should sit up and take notes? We say he is *Lord*, which means that he gets to tell us what to do, right?

What is it he tells us to "do not" do?

"Do not be anxious about your life."

When your Lord tells you to not be anxious, what should you do with that?

It's natural, as we shall see, to be afraid—completely rational and natural.

Can you remain fearful while growing in Jesus?

Dave says, "You need to grow in your faith and stop being afraid."

Fear destroys friendships, peace, health, and your life.

The love and grace of God bring light and peace to life, and as the good friend of Jesus also noted, "God is light, and in him is no darkness at all."[19]

Fear is a very dark place. We cannot, as those who take on the name of the Christ, dwell in darkness while claiming the indwelling of Emmanuel.

Let's talk.

An Expert in Fear

I consider myself to be an expert on fear. Not that I studied it in college or have a degree in fear-ology, but I spent too much of my life *living* in fear. From childhood on into my thirties, I would what-if and fret over just about everything.

By my late teens, I began having serious stomach pains and a weird, out-of-control feeling of fear—an event now known as a panic attack. At that time, I had never heard of such a thing. But I was experiencing them! I feared I was going crazy.

I had literally become afraid of fear. Let that sink in.

I decided to pursue being a military pilot, a really stupid choice for someone experiencing great fear and panic attacks. I didn't know it at the time, but that was a very *wise* choice—something the psychological profession calls exposure therapy. This is the process of determining what really scares you and doing it. Of course, my problem was that *life* scared me! I chose to pursue a bold life—with much trembling and tears.

But there was a temptation at one point presented by medicine. A wonder drug called Prozac came to the market, and so many people were singing its praises. It seemed to fix the panic and anxiety issues for a lot of people like me.

But then I knew, or at least was *fearful* (imagine that), that taking the drug would disqualify me as a military pilot. So I pushed through with only God and his people to lean on.

Long story short, God gave me the victory. It took years, but eventually I grew so weary of being fearful I decided death would be preferable.

I have loved life (and flying) ever since.

May I share some lessons our Lord taught me about conquering fear so that we can be the superheroes he intends—and we can deliver the world from their delusional state of fear-induced cruelty and hate?

The Raw Truth about Life on Earth

You should be afraid, *very* afraid.

That may sound strange in a chapter about conquering fear, but part of being courageous requires looking fear-producing situations straight on and *choosing* to embrace risk.

Risk is all around us, every moment of every day. It's risky to get out of bed in the morning and also risky *not* to get out of bed.

I had to get an ultrasound of my heart to check for a possible genetic defect that one of my children had. We were trying to see which side of the family it came from and possibly head off some trouble for my wife or me.

The technician doing the ultrasound was a sister of mine from my church family, and she did what sisters who love you do; she turned the monitor toward me and gave me a guided tour of my blood pump.

It was amazing.

It was honestly a bit scary.

In profile, it looked a lot flimsier and vulnerable than what I had imagined.

At the same time, I was full of joy and amazed at the design and *longevity* of this marvel inside of me. It had been pumping oxygenated blood through my system at that point for over five decades! What a marvelously designed and crafted piece of biomechanical machinery!

But it struck me. I was one missed tiny electrical impulse from death. Always had been, and I still was. I always would be.

My valves had a little leakage. "Typical for someone your age," she said. One of those incredible valves could just malfunction one day, just a bit, and I would be dead.

As I drove home from the appointment and an 18-wheeler swooshed past in the opposing lane, drifting toward me a bit, our combined velocity around 140 miles per hour, yet another way to die. I missed being killed by that one by about two feet (I was over next to the ditch, almost off the pavement). I have a dear friend who, in his family of five, lost his wife and two older children in a head-on with a big rig.

Death is always near the living.

Every time we drive our cars, we are feet or even inches from possible death.

I had lost friends and family to cancer, heart disease, car crashes, war, airplane crashes, strokes, old age, genetic conditions, and violence.

There are so many threats that can take us out, or the people we rely on, every day.

You can try to ignore that, but the natural response to the *real threats to life* we are exposed to every day is *fear.*

Only someone completely ignorant of that truth would not see that fear is the perfectly understandable and natural response to the visible and invisible threats to our lives and those that we value—every day.

But then our Lord Yeshua, the Messiah, made it clear that his enemy came to kill, steal, and destroy. Jesus was here, and is here, to give us an abundant life.[20]

Living in fear takes the joy out of life. To live in continual fear makes life horrible and tedious. Living in fear is dark and foreboding and reduces our health. Living in fear of death makes us more likely to die prematurely.

Fear is anti-abundance.

Fear is *anti-Christ!*

Can I be your Dave again? Living in fear forfeits your victory in Christ to Satan! While Jesus came to give us the abundant life,[21] Satan's goal is to steal, kill, and destroy.[22] There is no need to give Satan a "buy."

Can I just say that should not be!

Church, Much?

If you are a believer, you probably know very well that church is not something you go to. Yet we say it perhaps because we go to be *with* our church family—so there is an act of *going.*

Yet think about the Greek word *ecclesia,* from which *church* is derived. It means "the called-out ones."

In our culture today, we live in the most anxious, fearful, medicated, overstressed, addicted, lonely, suicidal, and sleep-deprived generation of people to ever walk the face of the earth. It is a terrible way to live, and the COVID debacle only made a really bad situation just horrendous. Suicide, depression, loneliness, fear, and substance abuse are way up.

It's too bad Christianity doesn't seem to offer much to hurting people, no?

My point is this—we are *called out!* We *are* to live abundantly and joyously even in, perhaps *especially during,* difficult times. As John the apostle specified, there was to be no darkness at all![23]

In times like these, with all the strife and stress of COVID, alleged oppression, inflation, war, violence, and terrorism, the church is to be a blinding light of peace, joy, and love.

Each believer is to be a beacon of brilliant courage and steadiness—inexplicable in their resolve to the nonbeliever. As Paul the apostle puts it, "The peace of God, which surpasses all understanding, will guard your hearts and minds in Christ Jesus."[24]

Just like the people who saw Jesus while he was on earth, there are two dominant responses. People either want what Jesus (or those in whom Jesus dwells) has, or they hate what they see—because their fear-induced hatred cannot stand being called out for their cowardice.

Our heritage, brothers and sisters, is a beautiful courage and peace that calls others to an abundant life in Christ. Our peace is to be beyond understanding; in other words, in times when no one expects peace, Christ's children should radiate it! Our lives, our response to the natural fears that the obvious threats to our lives present so clearly, is to glorify the source of our peace and draw wayward, lost souls to him.

However, this is not what the world is seeing today in the church. It. Is. Not.

Weird Things about Fear

I have a friend with a military special forces background. We flew together in my civilian airline job quite a bit, and over time, he shared some of the stories that he could (some stories are and likely will remain classified). He was an incredibly courageous, ferocious, and humble warrior. I would always try to pry more stories and details about how these *snake-eaters* (a popular term for these types of soldiers) do what they do.

Courageous—no question about it.

Except maybe in some situations, very fearful?

Part of airline flying are *line checks*. This is where either a governmental FAA representative or their designated agents ride with you to make sure you are flying the airplane in accordance with standard procedures. They are not that big of a deal; these folks just sit and watch you do your normal job, and usually if they see something wrong, they just tell you how you should have done it at the end of the flight. It really is a no-threat kind of event.

My special forces buddy and I were getting not a line check but even one level lower than that—a *quality check*. This was a guy riding with us from our company just to observe how well company procedures were working. It was absolutely no threat at all.

And my snake-eater buddy, a guy who would jump out of airplanes loaded with weapons and take the war to the enemy in unspeakably dangerous places—was clearly nervous. For all of his true and commendable courage in one area of life, this aspect of someone watching him fly the airplane really unnerved him.

That's the way fear is for most of us. I struggled for a long time with fear of everything, gained confidence of flying even into war zones with people shooting at me, yet still found myself fearful of confronting someone (even one of my own children) over something they had done wrong. Yes, a father afraid of confronting a child, for their own good.

Or I would have a chance to share my faith and stumble— because I was afraid of being seen as unsophisticated, or perhaps they would ask a question I couldn't answer.

Then I would go and strap on an airplane and blast off into the weather or gunfire with no fear at all.

I would ask myself, *Why do I do this aircraft thing, which really makes no difference, and yet not show courage where my God needs me to the most?*

I suspect from observation that we are all this way.

This Jesus person we claim to follow is a truly radical fellow. He made something clear to those who would follow him. To really *believe* in the Christ, we really should kick fear to the curb. If you are living daily with fear like I was, you have to be getting sick of it! Living in fear wears you out! What follows are some spiritual precepts from scripture on walking out of fear with Jesus.

It is not necessarily an easy or fast path, but it is worth the journey! I can testify that the really great stuff of the kingdom lies on the other side of fear!

The Stark Reality of Fear as a Saved Believer

In case you didn't pick this up earlier, you need to understand this. Living courageously can get you hurt or killed.

I've been flying airplanes now for forty-four years. Every now and then, someone asks, "Have you ever nearly crashed?" or "Have you ever been really scared?"

To be absolutely honest, absolutely yes. To both questions.

There are scary and dangerous situation stories that I might share with you, there are some I only discuss with fellow aviators, and there are a couple I don't even want to remember. They still make me unsettled, because it was almost always due to poor choices on my part that I nearly did myself (and others) in.

But here's the honest truth—living courageously is so worth it. I am thankful to still be alive, but all of the dangerous times also had their own reward. Combat is horrible, but overcoming the unique challenges of it is part of what makes you feel so alive and joined together with others who are with you. You grow through being challenged in life, and challenge often involves intensely fearful times that call on you to reach deep within yourself and especially upward toward God in order just to take the next grueling step—a step that could be your last.

Sebastian Junger, in his excellent book *Tribe: On Homecoming and Belonging*,[25] shares the story of a Bosnian teenager who was living and loving her friends. The girls would hide out in a subway tunnel from the shelling and shooting during the day while the teen boys went off to fight. At night, they would get together to eat, talk, dance, and just be together.

One day, while visiting her grandparents, their house was hit, and she was injured. Her parents arranged for her to be taken to a safe place to recover—in another country away from the war. She found herself lost and listless. She missed the intensity and closeness of life with her friends and soon made her way back to the war.

Living for safety in fear is not much of a life. The young Bosnian lady felt most alive connected with her friends in a war zone. We were put here to do more than eat, breathe, surf the internet, and poop. This is not a contest to see who can live the longest and have the best preserved, never-challenged, and safe corpse. If you never venture out to live courageously in the path of obedience our Lord has laid out before you, you will miss the epic adventure and joy he intends for us to experience.

Christianity *can* be deadly to your health. In many places in the world, giving your life to Christ involves many tears—because it means that likely your family will disown you, your community will shun you, and someone may kill you. From the first century onward, our faith in Jesus has been a faith to die for.

Step 1—Learn to See Death as a Friend

There is some heady theology in the New Testament book of Hebrews that talks about the *why* and *what* of Jesus's death on the cross. At one point though, he talks about perhaps one of the biggest fears for most people—death itself.

> Since therefore the children share in flesh and blood,
> he himself likewise partook of the same things, that
> through death he might destroy the one who has
> the power of death, that is, the devil, and deliver
> all those who through fear of death were subject to
> lifelong slavery.[26]

Unpacking this deep statement, the writer is sharing that Jesus's death and subsequent resurrection pretty much destroyed any power that the devil even has over us—even to the point of eliminating any need to fear death. We know, because of Jesus walking out of his own tomb under his own power and then ascending to heaven to sit at the right hand of God on his glorious throne, our future is entirely glorious!

He also notes something that if you are a fearful person you will grasp as truth. I sure did. Fear of death *is* lifelong slavery. Being afraid of dying compels a person to hold back, not take chances, play it safe, and otherwise miss the good things in life. Fear of death is a thief; it steals joy from the living. Do you want to be free?

Further, failing to conquer the fear of death on our part is to make what Jesus did on the cross and in coming out of the tomb under his own power null and void.

Paul, in his second letter to the Corinthians, explains the *how* of viewing death beautifully. Let's follow along with his line of reasoning:

> For we know that if the tent [our earthly body] is destroyed [we die] we have a building from God, a house not made with hands, eternal in the heavens. For in this tent we groan [life here is very good in some ways, but in other ways, meh.] longing to put on our heavenly dwelling, if indeed by putting it on we may be found not naked. For while we are in this tent, we groan, being burdened [if you aren't now, just wait, it's coming!]—not that we would be unclothed, but that we would be further clothed, so that what is mortal may be swallowed up in life.

Tents, burdens, and being swallowed up in life! When Paul speaks of being swallowed up in *life,* it seems to be directed toward a usage of the Greek word *zoe,* which means "the absolute fullness of life!" He is trying to tell us something that we really, really need to know.

The best stuff is on the other side of death!

This life has its joys for sure. Our Creator pronounced (right after the creation of man) that things were very good! But even on the best day, there is a niggling sense that the other shoe is about to drop. Someone will get sick or have an accident, a war will start, there will not be enough money to go around, or some other tragedy is lurking just around the corner.

At the very best, this great moment will come to an end.

19

Paul says the most excellent, best every day possible will be in the eternal and ultimate reality!

One experience I had helped me to frame this beautiful reality.

At the end of my air force pilot training, I was sent to survival school. It was a little over a week long, and the final event was about twenty-four hours in a prison camp.

As you would expect, this camp environment was based on a lot of real-life wartime prison camps and was designed to break you mentally, physically, and emotionally.

It wasn't that bad—because I kept a truth in my mind no matter what they did to me.

The clock is ticking!

They had to send us home when our time was up. They purposely kept us from seeing any clocks or watches while were there. They anticipated people like me with a serious coping strategy. They even played tapes of a verbal time hack broadcast where each minute the time changed in various directions by hours. It didn't faze me. I knew that each moment got me closer to the prison camp doors opening. I would go to my quarters for the night and the next day be on a flight home to be embraced in the arms of my beautiful and loving wife.

Can I suggest you meditate deeply on the teachings of scripture on death, heaven, and the assurances of Christ regarding our suffering? Getting *close* to death can be unsettling. You need to dwell on the Word of God, the promises of what lies beyond, to motivate you. The clock is always ticking on this life!

But death *is* a friend. The apostle Paul makes this clear:

> So we are always of good courage. We know that while we are at home in the body we are away from the Lord, for we walk by faith, not by sight. Yes, we are of good courage, and we would rather be away from the body and be at home with the Lord. So

whether we are at home or away, we make it our aim
to please him.[27]

God's Word makes it plain that beyond death is a future more
glorious than can be even partially grasped. We must grow in faith
in order to truly trust that what God's Word tells us is true. We must
learn to enter fear-producing conditions prayerfully, saying, "I trust
you, Lord. My life is yours."

Step 2—Learn to Stare at What Scares

Because of my history as the world's largest chicken, I have read
a lot of books on courage, the history of brave people, and of course
the biblical stories of God working through ordinary people like
you and me.

Several of our special forces soldiers have written books in
the past few years—and one freebie book I received due to some
e-book credits was from former Navy Seal David Webb in his book
Mastering Fear. He has an insightful strategy for dealing with fear:

> You may have seen the quote "What would you do
> if you were not afraid?" It's become one of those
> memes that people accept as divine revelation, as
> if it were handed down from Mount Sinai on stone
> tablets ... For me, though, here is a much more
> powerful question:
>
> "What would you do if you WERE afraid?"
>
> How would you deal with that fear? Would you let
> it stop you or propel you forward? Fear can be a set
> of manacles, holding you prisoner. Or it can be a
> slingshot, catapulting you on to greatness. Read the
> biographies of great men and women, and you find

21

> that people who accomplish great things typically
> do so not by denying or beating back their fears but
> by embracing them. Not seeing fear as the enemy
> but my making it their ally.[28]

Webb brings up an important truth—fear is not something to *pretend* doesn't exist. Nor is it something to allow to run your life.

Instead, do this.

First, when you recognize something is stimulating fear in you, look at the situation and ask why. What is it exactly that scares you? At its core, fear is a God-given mental-emotional response that *may* tell you that you or someone in your life is in danger. Is the threat real?

Much of the fear I experienced early in life was related to the condition of continual anxiety and stress in which I was living. I would be scared of a particular threat (maybe there were thunderstorms along the route of flight) and find myself worrying, obsessing, and anxious. But realistically, I had a few million dollars of training under my belt and a well-equipped aircraft and crew, and air traffic control also had radars and could help us navigate our way around the bad weather. In the event we still got in trouble, we routinely trained in the simulator on how to escape deadly wind shears.

In that case, by looking directly at what was bothering me, I could see that the risk of the moment was necessary, and I needed to just formulate my game plan for dealing with whatever came along. In other words, strap on the airplane and fly. Deal with the problem if it happens and when it happens—not with imaginary problems that have not happened.

If you fear dealing with people, if you feel tongue-tied or inadequate, learn to communicate better. You can find books and likely even some online videos to help you learn to become adept and comfortable at engaging others. But at some point, you have to put down the book and *start talking*. Once you do that, keep the momentum going. I recognized early in my adult years that energy begets energy, meaning that once you get rolling into something new, endeavor to keep it rolling. Make it a goal to talk with at least one person you do not know or know well every day you leave the house. Start the practice of having people over, especially neighbors or coworkers you do not know very well.

Step 3—Learn to See Death as a Comfortable Certainty

I like to recommend books.

We'll talk about why later, but one book that is surprisingly valuable to everyday courageous life is *Deep Survival: Who Lives, Who Dies, and Why* by Laurence Gonzales.[29] It is a riveting story of hellish situations in which some people find themselves—some who live and some who die. Gonzales notes the following problem with death and makes a vital recommendation on the starting point for living with death:

> Few of us believe our own mortality until we're face to face with it, and then some of us forget immediately afterward. So we have no way to prepare for what seems too remote a possibility. And as Christopher Burney, who was a prisoner of war at Buchenwald, said, "Death is word which presents no real target to the mind's eye." The best way to become a believer, short of dying, is to sit very quietly and contemplate those things.[30]

As we will discuss in the chapter on un-hacking our minds, this is perhaps one of the biggest strongholds of Satan on the church right now. We are so comfort addicted and enslaved to our dopamine reward system that sitting very quietly, as mentioned above, rarely happens for anyone. We are too on edge, agitated, and preoccupied to even begin to meditate on our own mortality.

But we must learn.

There is only one psalm in the Bible attributed to Old Testament hero Moses. In it, he gives us something critical to know about humankind even in his time: "Teach us to number our days, so that we can get a heart of wisdom."[31]

Dave has a word for the church today. If there is any indicator that we as God's children lack and need a heart of wisdom, it is the impotence and fear characterizing the western church today.

Throughout God's Word, there are true stories showing how God works through people to accomplish his plan. But quite frankly, the invitation is nearly always terrifying and potentially deadly in nature.

A shepherd boy steps into combat with a huge, experienced warrior-giant (with a slingshot and five rocks?).

An orphaned girl is taken from her home and put into training to be in a pagan king's harem—and saves her nation.

We need to be really clear about the call of Jesus; however, it can cost you your life.

It can cost you your life.

It can cost you your life.

Did you hear me? Dave here, following Jesus, living the abundant life that Jesus came to bless us with. *It can cost you your life.*

Do not be deceived. Following Jesus and joining him in the battle against Satan makes you a target. Sometimes Satan and his demons home in on you with a laser-guided, rocket-propelled bomb and vaporize your little pink, crunchy tent (your body).

It is the reason Jesus told his followers to "count the cost."

It can cost you *everything.*

Perfect love casts out fear.

Dave out …

CHAPTER 3

If It Hadn't Been for My Parents

I think she is growing up, and so begins to dream dreams, and have hopes and fears and fidgets, without knowing why or being able to explain them.
—Louisa May Alcott

Aging is a necessary but insufficient requirement for growing up. There are immature old people and appropriately mature young people.
—Henry Cloud

If you are to be, you must begin by assuming responsibility.
—Antoine de Saint-Exupery

Do not be overcome by evil, but overcome evil with good.
—Paul the apostle

~~~~~~

When I was young, my dad was my hero.
I also prayed that he would die.

Pretty drastic for a ten-year-old.

I loved my dad, as did most of the people in my town. He was funny, talented, and outgoing. For many years of my life, I wanted to be just like him. He hung out with country music stars and TV personalities and could make friends with just about anybody he ran into. He wrote three books of poetry, his album covers for musicians won numerous awards, and he was in a movie and the TV series *HeeHaw*.

He was a small-town hero, and he was my hero.

As his health deteriorated, someone asked my wife, "Has Steve been grieving his dad?"

"He's been grieving his dad all his life" was her very observant response.

You see, for all our little-town world knew, my dad was an awesome human being.

He absolutely *sucked* as a father. My sisters and I were pretty messed up by growing up around someone who was a narcissistic, selfish, womanizing, alcohol-and-drug-abusing, and probably mentally ill person.

He was never much into being a father to the children he had produced.

It created a lot of serious issues for me and my sisters. After he died earlier this year, we got together to get his house ready for auction—and we shared some of the ways who he was messed up who we are.

The reality is, and this has been researched thoroughly, bad parenting can create lifelong challenges for us as adults. The work of Bowlby and others on *attachment theory* in particular shows that even from our earliest days, the behavior of our mother profoundly impacts the development of our view of the world and ourselves.

It is unfortunately true that mothers (and fathers) often pass on the damage from their parents on to their own children.

You, like me, may have been greatly harmed by one or both of your parents. Or maybe you were harmed because one or both of your parents abandoned you. The list of damage we receive from messed-up and selfish people who reproduce without embracing the sacred responsibility of that honor can be extensive.

But here's the deal.

We can live our entire lives blaming our parents for our current situation.

In our current culture where nearly everyone can have a platform from which to share and declare faux wisdom, it has been rather popular (and unfortunately acceptable) to proclaim to the world, "Don't tell me to get over it!"

Whether the issue is trauma from poor parenting, anxiety, or past trauma, even counselors now embrace this "don't tell me" mentality.

Can I be your Dave? As someone who has struggled with bad parenting, anxiety, panic attacks, trauma, and addiction, can I offer a course away from flying into a mountain?

Get over it.

But here's the truth. You likely can't get over it on your own (nor can you with just counseling help either), and even if you do "get over it," there will be a valuable and precious scar for the rest of your life. In dark moments, you may pull back, or Satan may put before you, the hurt you experienced from less than perfect parents. But you need to get over it. You need to start living the truth of what God says about you. You need to be who our Lord knows you are.

"Getting over it" is the path God led me down. It is a very difficult path, and it is the beautiful path.

The scar is beautiful too.

From the bitter weeping of the damaged place can come the greatest of joys, the most nurturing compassion, and profound gratitude.

But will you accept the challenge to not give another day to living as a victim? Can you take a lifelong walk with Yeshua to become a victor?

It's tough, and it is beautiful ...

Your Parents Are Not God

"It seems that girls can overcome a bad mother, but it's harder when the father is bad," shared my second daughter. I asked her why she thought that was. "I think maybe it is because we talk about Father God—a bad earthly father messes up your image of who God is," she replied.

Perhaps the most essential step in overcoming parental wounds is to gain a truer understanding and a more complete image of who God is.

In *Thrive: The Biblical Essential of Conquering Trauma and Being Resilient*, I shared the transformational moment for the Old Testament character Job. He had lost all of his adult children, his servants, all of his possessions, and his health in a very brief period of time. He was angry with God, though not disloyal, but he wanted answers.

One thing happened that utterly changed Job from cursing God to praise. It happened when God came to Job and his friends in a whirlwind and surrounded them with his presence:

> If Job could sit down with us and share what he learned … I believe this would be one of the two main points he would grab us by the shoulders and shout at us. Job knew a lot about God, and he tried to serve him as best he could, given what he knew. But in his encounter with the God who spoke to him from a whirlwind, Job discovered something amazing.
>
> The God whose presence enveloped and overwhelmed him in the whirlwind was completely captivating compared to the smaller version of God he had served earlier. It wasn't that Job was following a false God, it was just that his view of God was entirely inadequate and beneath the majesty of the one true God. In this whirlwind experience, Job's relationship took an exponential leap of knowledge—from knowing about God to experiencing the reality of who God is!

As Job sat there in the whirlwind, his old view of
God was shattered. His high view of his own self
also was utterly destroyed.[32]

Without a whirlwind containing the Creator of the universe
being available to us, how do we experience the Father who loves us
with a perfect love?

There are probably a lot of ways to do this, but here are a few I
want to share with you as your brother:

1.   *Convo with God, regularly.* I've called this process various things,
from Bible reading, devo time, or armor-up time—but I've settled
lately on something else. When I wake up before my wife and sit
down with God and his Word, and then later say good morning to
her, she'll ask, "What have you been doing?"

My reply now is "Meeting with God." Or "Having coffee
with God."

The point is I need to say something that reminds me of what it
is I am striving to do. I am trying to sit with our Creator and have a
conversation. He speaks through his Word, and so reading the Bible
is a big part of it.

But you can read the Word with the "I need to read the Bible"
mentality and get nothing from it. So I "have a convo" with God.

Whatever *you* call it, remember that God's Word is a revelation
of God—which does mean that he inspired it, but more importantly,
it reveals through its stories, poetry, law, and letters who he is!

It reveals his heart, what he desires in the way we treat one
another and ourselves, and how he views each person on earth. It
shows his beauty—something those of us who were perhaps harmed
by earthly fathers (and their designees, our mothers, or whoever
raised us) really need to understand.

Of course, God reveals himself to us in other ways, through the
glory of his creation, by speaking through others, and through the
leading of the Holy Spirit.

29

The problem you must deal with though is if you do not have a very strong knowledge of the Bible, you will likely be led astray by the spirit.

Notice that I referred to the little *s* spirit.

The big truth God reveals to us is revealed from cover to cover in his Word but is specifically spelled out in Malachi where it says, "For I the LORD do not change."[33]

If we do not *know* the Lord God pretty well from scripture, then we will be easily deceived either by our own selfish spirit (where we give "God's approval" to our own selfish desires and arrogant thoughts) or to demonic spirits, when they sell us a bill of goods we want to hear.

In effect, if you do not know the Bible, you do not know whether or not the "spirit leading" you think you perceive is biblical.

If you believe that Bible is the inerrant Word of God, then treat it like it is.

Back to Malachi. God dealt with shallow believers when he said,

> You have wearied the LORD with your words. But you say, "How have we wearied him?" By saying "Everyone who does evil is good in the sight of the LORD, and he delights in them." Or by asking, "Where is the God of justice?"[34]

We will likely not overcome our tainted views of God the Father unless we come to know the heart of the one true Father revealed through his Word.

Have a daily convo with God. Preferably make him the first priority in the morning.

2.   Develop close relationships with a few close brothers/sisters in Christ. This is the "our, not my" group, remember? Some of the greatest growth toward seeing God more clearly as he is occurred because of brothers and sisters I spent a lot of time with, and during some of those times, we shared God.

We shared what we were learning in our own times with God. We shared times when we perceived God was working in our lives. We shared books we were reading that taught us about God. We asked deep questions and shared doubts, fears, and desires.

In other words, we did the to "one another's" of scripture. We grew in our knowledge of God together and still are. We have held and continue to hold one another accountable in our endeavors to pursue a strong relationship with our Creator.

We trust God and these closest brothers and sisters with who we really are—warts and all.

And through this process, God reveals himself in his glory as we are able to endure it.

3.   *Ask God to reveal his glory to you.* Yes, do this, but be warned; this can be breathtaking, scary, and shocking. This is as it must be.

When Moses asked to see God's glory, our Father obliged but had to limit it a bit. Moses asked, "Please, show me your glory."[35]

The Father obliged but let Moses know that he could not endure seeing all of him at once:

> "I will make all my goodness pass before you and will proclaim before you my name 'The LORD.' I will be gracious to whom I will be gracious, and will show mercy on whom I will show mercy. But you cannot see my face, for man shall not see me and live."[36]

I cannot tell you for sure all of the ways in which God will show the glory of his goodness to you—but be prepared. He is far more pure, holy, powerful, good, and unspeakable *other* than you think!

Ask God to show you his glory as you are able to receive it. We all need this!

4. *Start your day with the Lord. Then walk with expectancy.* Perhaps I'm hitting that first part again, but it is for a reason. You can do your time with God anytime you want, but from personal experience, I have found it valuable to start with him and include in my time speaking with him, "Lord, help me to see you working and give me the courage to join in where you show me to" or something along that line.

Jesus showed this pattern in his own life when he said, "The Son can do nothing of his own accord, but only what he sees the Father doing. For whatever the Father does, the Son does likewise."[37]

Although this is a specific example applying to Jesus, my perception from dwelling in the Word is that our Father has always been working among people and inviting his devoted children to join in the work.

This has been a thrilling part of my life and one that helps me to see the beauty and the love of the Father who will never fail me.

How Does This Solve Parent Issues?

As mentioned earlier, the first step to overcoming attachment or traumatic damage from our parents or whoever served as our parents is to begin to see our Father God more accurately as he is. I cannot speak for you, but I felt utterly rejected by my father, which made me feel unworthy of the love of others.

If you choose to start meeting with God first thing in the morning, understanding that he desires and is happy to be with you, and then go through your day *with* him, you will begin to see that *he* really does love you as the perfect Father. He desires to shower you with the love, mercy, and grace that he abounds in—and to convince you that you have no need to feel less than, worth less than others, or unworthy of respect.

He respects you! After all, he made you. You're some of his best work!

Further, Jesus's good friend John shared the following beautiful truth that this four-step discipline will help you to *know* is true:

> See what kind of love the Father has given to us, that we should be called the children of God; and so we are. The reason the world does not know us is that it did not know him. Beloved, we are God's children now, and what we will be has not yet appeared; but we know that when he appears we shall be like him, because we shall see him as he is. And everyone who thus hopes in him purifies himself as he is pure.[38]

There is so much here—you and I *are* God's children.

But pay attention to that truth about the world not knowing us because it doesn't know him. Is it true for those of us with parental wounds that we don't know us because we do not know him? Our concept of God the Father was tainted by our imperfect parents, and perhaps by our well-intentioned church families as well?

In my case, both were true. I felt rejected by and disappointing to my earthly father. He was cool, attractive, capable, and handsome. I was none of that. My church family treated me wonderfully but had inherited and embraced a very legalistic perspective on God—and it just reinforced that my heavenly Father was just as disapproving, disappointed, and ashamed of me as my earthly father. I was baptized when I was twelve, determined to be a good boy and show my heavenly Father, who I feared greatly, that I was worthy of his love and of membership in heaven. By age fifteen, I was so entwined in sin I *knew* I was hell bound.

I left God and his church for a few years and tried to live as an atheist. During that time, I decided to disprove the Bible—since it obviously couldn't be true. After a about a year and a half of study and hard drinking, porn, and failed attempts at romantic relationships, I hit rock bottom, and the Bible stood as solid as an anvil being pounded by an eight-ounce ball peen hammer.

I crawled back to God.

It was a long journey, from age twenty-two to about forty, before I reached a point of joy and absolute assurance of God's adoration of me, and I wrote my earthly father (and mother) letters of nothing but gratitude for *all* they had done.

You see, I realized something as I applied the four disciplines above. I had become a very strong, very loved, very happy, very secure, emotionally healthy, and relationally blessed son. Had I had a more loving earthly father, I likely would not have hugged my heavenly Father quite so strongly. I have never let go.

At a certain point in this journey, I was reading the Gospel of John, the part where Jesus says some hard things, and a lot of followers just turn around and leave. He looks at his closest disciples and asks if they are going to leave too. Peter says something that brought me to tears of joy and gratitude:

> Lord, to whom shall we go? You have the words of
> eternal life, and we have believed, and have come to
> know, that you are the Holy One of God.[39]

I was so thankful that through this beautiful and painful journey with my Lord, he had brought me to the same place. I knew that although there would be some tough days ahead, moments of doubt, and moments when I would fail, I would never again let go of my most beautiful Father.

Through so many mornings spent together talking, through his gradually showing me the beauty and glory of his goodness, through seeing him working with me and through the magnificent brothers and sisters he so generously placed in my life, I was convicted of his absolute and faithful love for me.

You *can* be a victor instead of a victim. You *can* get over it, so to speak.

Not alone. God never intended that.

Paul beautifully describes the nature of walking with our Lord with expectancy:

> But thanks be to God, who in Christ always leads us in triumphal procession, and through us spreads the knowledge of him everywhere.

Triumphal procession can be the legacy of your life. Believe what God says is true of you!

Dave out ...

CHAPTER 4

Un-Hack Your Life

The difference between technology and slavery is that
slaves are fully aware that they are not free.
—Nassim Nicholas Taleb

Things are in the saddle
And ride mankind
—Ralph Waldo Emmerson

Wisdom cries aloud in the street, in the markets she raises her voice; at
the head of the noisy street she cries out; at the entrance of the city gates
she speaks; "How long, O simple ones, will you love being simple?"
—Solomon, king of Israel

In 2000, Microsoft Canada reported that the average human had
an attention span of twelve seconds; by 2013 that number had
fallen to eight seconds. (According to Microsoft, a goldfish, by
comparison, has an average attention span of nine seconds.)
—Adam Alter[40]

Do you feel like life is getting away from you? Do you look at your schedule and see "white time" where nothing is scheduled, but then at the end of the week, you see no progress toward what is important, and you're not sure what happened to that time?

That was my experience a few years ago. I was fortunate enough to have a really good job that routinely offered long stretches of days off and even time off while working in nice hotels—plenty of time to do the things that mattered to me the most.

Yet I experienced that same "what happened" with my off time so regularly that I finally decided to test something out, and what I found was *transformative* to my life!

I've taught and shared this amazing switch to a number of people, and they have reported a life turnaround in several cases.

Would you like to know the secret to getting the most precious nonrenewable resource on earth to work for you? That's your *time* you know!

Not only that, but do you find yourself having trouble relaxing? Are your shoulders tense, muscles aching, mind endlessly flowing with worrisome thoughts, seeking comfort from food, games, or something else?

That's caused by the same thing.

Let me share what I discovered in my own life, then let you in on the secret path to victory in getting done what needs to be done through redeeming your time.

Hacked Me

By 2018, I had started a number of books and never gotten very far with any of them. I had a huge list of things I needed to get done; it just seemed to get longer all the time.

As I mentioned, I had a bunch of white space on my calendar in which I supposedly could write or attack my imposing lists, but finally in late 2018, I got sick of the whole situation.

I had just finished my master's degree in marriage and family therapy and had done very well at disciplining myself in research and writing. I wanted to keep that momentum going and write my first book. But I was concerned about my disappearing *off time*, so I developed a plan.

I knew deep inside that my smartphone and other electronic

devices were leaching my time away, so I developed a plan for an *electronic-media fast*. The specific plan I followed is in the appendix, if you care to follow this path.

I removed all noncommunication, nonessential programs and turned off all notifications from my smartphone. Then when I sat down to write, I put the phone in airplane mode and out of arm's reach. I would write in forty-five-minute to one-hour blocks and then turn the phone on during lunch or at the end of the writing day. I only checked email twice a day, and I avoided my phone within an hour of waking up or two hours of going to bed.

The funny thing was, in securing a publisher, my publishing assistant, before I had really begun writing, asked when she could expect to receive the manuscript.

I answered, "Eight weeks."

She could not restrain her laughter. She said that would be great but not very realistic. Most people take a whole lot longer than that!

She was right. I was being unrealistic.

I did it in six weeks!

Without the continual distraction of dings, swiping, email, social media, games, and phone calls regarding my soon expiring automobile warranty, I cranked out my first book (and it was selected for publication) in six weeks!

I had managed to turn my white time into achieving a lifetime goal of writing a manuscript that was published.

An Odd Thing Happened

One weird thing that happened in that six weeks is that I gained five pounds. But because of some of my earlier studies, I suspected I knew at least some of the connection between my weight gain and getting control of the electronic gadgets in my life—dopamine.

Smartphones and the programs on them are designed to maximize engagement time through stimulating dopamine, a feel-good or motivation-related chemical in our brains. This is a science that program and hardware designers use in order to maximize the amount of attention users give to their devices.

It makes money—lots of money.

As one point of reference, one of the video games that was huge for a while was (and still is to a degree) *Candy Crush Saga*. During its highest use time, it was bringing in more than $600,000 in revenue each day. Its developer raked in billions of dollars in revenue, and most of the players were *women,* which was very unusual for a video game at the time.[41] To describe how the game works seems strange in print—it doesn't sound very engaging written on the page! But that is the point; the game designers know how to create an addictive experience for players that keeps them playing for far longer than such a worthless activity deserves.

Candy Crush Saga is just one example of how the merchants of the digital age can hack your brain and steal your life! Such games, email, texting, even a program I use for my regular job are actually well designed to stimulate the chemical dopamine, so they cleverly keep you on the hook for more.

Back to the weight gain I experienced when I got my phone under control. Sugar is another dopamine producer. In fact, it is so potent that it is surprising how many things contain sugar and how much we consume!

From 2010, the generally accepted consumption of sugar per American was 150 pounds total, with sixty-six of that being *added* sugar. Added sugar refers to the druglike refined versions of sugar—which are addictive and dopamine producing. The rest is in the naturally occurring fructose form, which the body handles differently.[42] By contrast, in the early 1800s, the typical American ate about two pounds!

Dr. Robert Lustig has published several books, but perhaps his best one-stop resource to date is *The Hacking of the American Mind: The Science Behind the Corporate Takeover of Our Bodies and Brains.*[43] In it, he makes a powerful contention that *sucrose* (refined sugar of any type) is not nutritional (i.e., not required by the body

39

to function), is addictive, and therefore should be considered to be more along the line of a drug, such as the other white powder, *cocaine*. He points out that the impact of sugar on dopamine receptors through continual overstimulation is very similar; too much continual dopamine stimulation from any source results in *downregulation*, which usually causes a person to consume more of the drug/substance/program to achieve the same good feelings.[44]

The bad news about long-term downregulation of dopamine receptors is that after too long a period, they *die*. Too much dopamine kills your ability to feel pleasure. Dopamine receptors will not regenerate once they have gone away.

More bad news is that serotonin, the contentment chemical that also helps us rest well at night, is being crowded out by our high-sugar, high–electronic device, and overly sexualized society (sex is a major dopamine producer as well). This leads to what I perceive as a generalized sense of anxiety, overstimulation, and an inability to rest. The quote from the start of the chapter on the average attention span makes sense in light of the high levels of dopamine stimulation so many of us are under. We cannot pay attention because we are so agitated—and we choose not to exercise discipline in choosing to pay attention.

We've been hacked.

Tech philosopher Paul Graham said it best about the dangers we are facing today:

> The world is more addictive than it was 40-years ago ... more things we like mean more things we have to be careful about ... most people won't, unfortunately.[45]

In the same article, he well articulates the challenge we are presented in making a choice about what our normal mode of living is going to be, especially for those of us who know that we were created to live in an abundant[46] way:

The two senses in which one can live a normal
live will be driven even further apart. One sense of
"normal" is statistically normal: what everyone else
does. The other sense we mean when we talk about
the normal operating range of a piece of machinery:
what works best ... already someone trying to live
well would seem eccentrically abstemious in most
of the U.S.[47]

He is so right. Our dopaminergic system was designed by
our Creator for good, but the continual overstimulation of it by
electronic media, devices, games, tattoos (yep, they produce it too),
high-glycemic (sugary) foods, and other popular thrills in their high
abundance and normal acceptance lead to a population that is not
content, continually agitated, and extremely unhealthy. The blue
light emitted from electronic screens tells our body to emit wakeful
chemicals, the ongoing dopamine hits leave us wanting more, and
we are exposed to crises and trauma far remote from our circle of
impact. Is it any wonder we cannot sleep?

While it is normal to walk around with your head buried in a
screen, eating high-sugar foods and drinking sodas, isolated from
real, human face-to-face contact, it is not normal from the standpoint
of how you were designed to thrive! We are image bearers of our
amazing God, and the Creator God is the three-in-one *trinitarian*
being—he is relational to his core.

Therefore, we are relational! We are meant to be in one another's
lives and faces, touching one another daily. *Virtual connection sucks.*
We need one another, and we need to be connecting with our Creator,
not with a device running a dopamine-hit-generating program!

The societal normal is abnormal when we consider the
marvelously connected and rhythmic way in which we were designed
to live. These devices, our food/drink choices, and our fear are
killing us.

We were not meant to live like this.

The Phone Is a Tool?

I said at an earlier time that a phone is just a tool, and we have to learn to use it properly.

I repent.

I was wrong.

It *is* something that is here to stay.

But it is more than a tool.

I was convicted of this by author Nicholas Carr's fascinating book *The Shallows: What the Internet Is Doing to Our Brains.*[48] In his book, he quotes Marshall McLuhan, who coined the phrase "the medium is the message" in the 1950s. McLuhan was primarily analyzing the impact of broadcast television and radio, and at the time, there was much concern about the impact of the *messages* being sent on these somewhat new but increasingly present devices in American homes. Carr notes that McLuhan was actually rather prophetic and correct; we should be less concerned with the messages conveyed and more fully understand that the device (i.e., the radio or television) was more important itself! It was the device that would bring about a far more significant change to the way we lived and thought. Carr shares that McLuhan "prophesied … the dissolution of the linear mind."[49]

McLuhan was right about the medium (the technology) being more important than the message. Television and radio did more than just change our society through the messages; it changed the way America (and other countries) *lived.* Instead of getting together with friends on the front porch and talking, families increasingly chose to stay home to watch their shows. As the number of channels increased, community life became deprioritized. Church meetings became shorter because the television provided something to do on the evenings. Televised sports took the place of community leagues, and instead of sitting in the bleachers with neighbors and chatting while supporting the hometown boys and girls, we sat in our own living rooms, and our neighbors became, too often, unknown.

The television did indeed change the way we think and our ability to pay attention. There are constraints on programming that require more a summary presentation of a story rather than great detail. Keeping people engaged involves more emotion than thought; things have to happen quickly and even explosively. The linear thinking mind has indeed been *undone,* now swapped for a fast-paced, quickly changing, emotion-based reasoning that lacks depth.

Listen, the medium *does* matter. Bad programming programs us! A bad message can pull us away from God if not met with a heart and mind prepared with truth.

But much of our isolation in society today started with the mediums of television and radio long ago. Within our homes, we became increasingly self-sufficient at amusing ourselves rather than connecting with others as we were designed to do. It is vital to recognize that the word *amuse* means "without the mind"! Our devices mindlessly distract, agitate, and placate us while keeping us from the life-giving rhythms of connection, creation, rest, and recreation.

The smartphone has been more transformative than even the television. Now you can be in public, with people, and still be utterly isolated. Most of us have seen a group of people at one table in a restaurant where no one is interacting. Everyone is facedown on their phones.

Not only that but the type of information coming through the smartphone has increased anxiety and fear and produced a general inability to communicate with real people.

No, the smartphone is not just a tool. It determines the nature of our society, and we must be wise and in control of it if we are to live the abundant superheroic life that the Christ intends.

Upended Intent for Flourishing

The impact of ever-present media and its tendency to isolate us, to prevent us from deeply thinking, to string us out on a never-ending flow of dopamine hits—it runs counter to the loving way in which our Creator made our natural environment to nurture us. Perhaps it was never intentional on the part of the designers of this new tech (or maybe it was; I'm not so sure Satan wasn't behind all of it), but you could not have designed a more efficient way of causing misery, suffering, anxiety, and a lack of peace in the creatures God so lovingly gave life to.

How do we restore the environment of nurture and grace in which God intended his children to live—not in some utopian sense but in the sense that even in the severest season of testing and suffering, we can go to the rock of our salvation and find comfort and strength?

I would suggest that we look at two places to start a journey back toward peace.

First, look at the way that God designed our world to interact and nourish us.

Second, look at the way God lived when he took up residence in a human body—in the person we English speakers generally know as Jesus.

Camping and Staying up All Night

When my kids were young, we would go camping. My wife wasn't really into camping, and I figured since we homeschooled and she was with them nearly *all* the time, it would be good for me to give her a break.

Of course, with their mom away, the kids knew they could get away with some things that their mother wouldn't let them do. One of those requests that came up on occasion was "Dad, can we stay up as late as we want?"

I always answered, "Yes!"

They were nearly always asleep by eight thirty! And I knew it would happen.

We did tent camping, and although we carried flashlights, I did not invest in any other significant campsite lighting; we just had a fire. That wood would glow a gentle orangish-red, crackling softly as the world got quiet. The bugs and frogs would begin their harmonious nightly "Symphony in G" (Goodness, that is), and one by one, my little ones, and even the not so little ones, would put themselves to bed.

You see, without artificial light in the blue spectrum, our bodies go into *rest* mode! I never had to force my kids to go crawl in their sleeping bag. The system our Creator designed to help us rest worked every time.

Can you see even at this simple level where this is going? If we were to attempt to return to a more God-designed home environment (lower light levels, no blue light–emitting screens, and soft sounds), we would naturally get more a better quality and quantity of much-needed rest.

Further, much has been made of the American diet. Food that is profitable and cheap to produce often makes us either too agitated to sleep or causes our blood sugar to drop in such a short time that we end up hungry and awake at awkward hours of the morning.

If we were to eat food in a form closer to what God designed it in, and with a lot less sugar, refined carbs, caffeine, and, well, you get the picture, we would rest better, have higher and more consistent energy, and our minds would think more clearly.

In fact, after my electronic fast and in wake of my weight gain, I got off of sugar for a year and a half. I was just curious as to how that would work, but I knew I was eating way too much of that white powder.

What I experienced surprised me.

First, within a short time, I found myself sleeping more soundly and often through the night without waking up. I didn't anticipate that, but it is a well-documented benefit of a low or no-sugar diet.

Second, my thought life improved. I could think more clearly, remember things better, and sustain mental effort for a longer period of time without getting brain fog. In my job as an airline pilot, which is primarily a thinking type of job (with a smattering of hand-eye coordination thrown in), that was a huge safety benefit.

Another strange thing occurred—once again totally unexpected. About three months into my sugar fast, my wife and I took a trip for her birthday to Abingdon, Virginia. There is a great casual bicycle trail there, "The Creeper Trail." It is named after an old coal- and worker-hauling train that went up and down the hills slowly (thus, the "Creeper" moniker), but that train bed has since been converted into a beautiful and fun bike path. It is over thirty miles long, the first seventeen of which are mostly downhill—thus no tight spandex required (my kind of ride).

After we rode the trail and cleaned up, we went to a beautiful outdoor patio–style local restaurant. The weather was perfect, I was with the woman I love—there was no stress. Yet I noticed my shoulders were tight and lifted, like someone was about to hit me, and I was bracing.

Through my getting off of sugar and continual electronic stimulation, I became aware that I had been living in this constant agitated and tense state. Even my body was contracted, nearly constantly. I no longer knew how to relax! From this day forward, I knew I had to stay on this path of seeking to live in the manner my Creator intended for me—so that I would be capable and resilient no matter what situations he needed me to be in.

Who Does That Jesus Character Think He Is?

I've long been distressed over most of the Pharisees in Jesus's day. They put a lot into their seeking of God. They studied the Law, they strove for religious excellence, and they tried diligently to codify and even build a hedge around every command so as to not get sideways with God.

Yet when God stood right beside them, shoulder to shoulder, they could not recognize him. Other than Nicodemus and hopefully a handful more, the prophecies Yeshua of Nazareth fulfilled should have made it clear who he was. And yet the artificial but well-intentioned world of the Pharisees kept them from recognizing God in the flesh when he was close enough to hug.

How incredibly tragic.

Yet, do we do the same?

Do we *claim* the name of Christ and yet fail to see who he was and how he lived when he was in human form?

One thing you can say about him—even though he was fully God, he respected and lived in a way that *showed* us that we need to respect our physical and emotional limitations.

On one well-known occasion, he was teaching a large group of people, and they had been there for a while. The area was remote. You likely know the story. He takes the small lunch of a young boy and feeds five thousand people[50] with it, and there were leftovers to spare. The scripture tells us something interesting—something we can learn from God in human form that would greatly benefit humans in human form:

> Perceiving that they were about to come and take
> him by force to make him King, Jesus withdrew
> again to the mountain by himself.[51]

Unpacking this, our God the Son in human flesh spends the day teaching and works a substantial miracle as well. The people are thrilled (as it turns out, many for the wrong reason) and desire to make him king.

Think about it. Jesus is coming to announce the kingdom of heaven. This is a perfect opportunity to build a platform and a following.

His response? He *withdrew* from them quietly, and the writer John adds the important note that he went *again* to mountain *by himself!*

The Savior of us all is *demonstrating with his feet that we need time alone with God to meditate and process the thoughts of our heart.*

We cannot, any more than our Savior could be when in human form, be *on* all the time! He had a huge day of teaching and feeding people. He took time to go get quiet and commune with the Father.

Back to simpler times in the world, before electric lighting, television, and certainly before always connected smart devices with blue light–emitting screens, there naturally came a time when the world got darker and quieter and there was less to do. People were forced to sit with their thoughts, talk with friends and family, talk with God—and give order to turmoil within.

Jesus came into the world to be King but not in the sense these people wanted. They just wanted the free bread and fish. His kingdom was far more substantial, not of earth although in place on earth today—but a kingdom of the heart, the spirit, and the Spirit of God.

Much to unpack, but if God in the flesh takes time to rest after working and takes time to experience solitude in order to connect with the Father and process the deep matters of life, what should we created and beloved children do?

Take a Sabbath

One of my military buddies sent me a link to TV talk by a famous doctor. My friend was very amused. This doctor was sharing that he had researched and thought it was a profound idea that we shouldn't work all the time. Perhaps we should all strive, he shared, to take one day off—one out of every seven, perhaps?

Brilliant. Too bad our Creator never said anything like that!

In my faith tradition, much has been made of the truth that the Old Law does not apply to us, and that is true to an extent. But what is often missed is that our God does not change; eternal principles of truth and justice that he declares are always true and just.

And of course, the principle of the Sabbath rest precedes the giving of the Old Law:

> The heavens and earth were finished, and all the host of them. And on the seventh day God finished his work that he had done. So God blessed the seventh day and made it holy, because on it God rested from all his work that he had done in creation.[52]

God made a Sabbath rest special from that day, and he later clarified something important when he handed down the covenant to Israel:

> Remember the Sabbath day, to keep it holy. Six days you shall work, and do all your work.[53]

In my other job, a lot of my friends are retiring. I have asked a few of them what they plan on doing after retirement, and the answer is often, "Nothing," or "Fish and play golf!"

Not a good plan. We were put here, looking back to what is the normal for the machine mentioned earlier, to work. We are to work six days. We are designed to function best and be our most holistically healthy when we have meaningful work to do.

But then the Sabbath, the issue of resting, is far more than a command. It is a state of *normal* that requires each of us to look at all of our needs, responsibilities, and desires and then say to our Creator, "I trust you."

The reason we so often do not rest and become so agitated is because we fear not having enough, not being thought of by others as enough, or failing due to lack of effort. Honoring God through saying, "I rest today," also implies complete trust that our heavenly Father is capable and *will* provide for our needs.

I do not necessarily contend that you must rest on Saturday. One only needs to travel to Israel to see how the Sabbath can be transformed from a time of peace to an ugly burden to be dreaded. (For example, a Sabbath elevator stops at every floor. Some folks are afraid that pushing a floor button would anger God—a tragic and blasphemous view of God!) I often, because of my work schedule, take a Monday as my rest.

Trust that God has your back, your front, your stomach, and your heart. Rest.

Jesus Worked with All His Heart

I love the story of the Samaritan woman at the well. It shows how God views anyone, in spite of labels that we might apply to one another.

But there is an important scene. The disciples left Jesus at the well to go into town and get food. During this time, Jesus has this life-changing conversation with this poor woman whose life is a huge, hot mess. When the disciples return, they are surprised that he is talking with a Samaritan woman (a big Jewish no-no for a rabbi), and they urge him to eat some food.

His answer tells us his where his heart was with regard to the work his Father had sent him to do. "I have food to eat that you do not know about."[54] His work was so important to him that while he was talking to the woman and the people she led to him, *he was full.* His work of reaching lost souls satisfied him as much as anything he could have put in his mouth.

But his disciples were confused by the statement, so he unpacked it more: "My food is to the will of him who sent me and to accomplish his work."

Understand, in the eyes of his Jewish disciples, the Samaritans were *dogs,* and I don't mean pets. They were like mangy, dirty, and untouchable enemies. Why would a good rabbi consider working with them at all? It wasn't even honorable.

That's a big problem for many believers today. We may talk about *doing all as unto the Lord,*[55] but in reality, we only want to do something big that makes us look important to others. We have in our culture a strong desire for celebrity. A job that is low level or even not seen (i.e., being a good mother, father, or cleaning house) is seen as *beneath* the requirement of doing "as unto the Lord" because it doesn't seem to bring us glory.

Jesus sure didn't see it like his disciples did. In fact, he would, just before his crucifixion, wash the feet of them all—a menial job normally done by household servants.

Get the message? If you are naming the name of the Christ, do *everything* with vigor and the best attitude you can muster. As the foot washer from heaven noted, "One who is faithful in a very little is also faithful in much."[56]

If you are waiting to shine in a big role in God's kingdom, it may never be entrusted to you if you aren't hitting it hard in the small and hidden duties he has given you every day!

Be like Jesus. Put your all into your work!

Jesus Connected

As mentioned earlier, we are a lonely bunch in America and much of the rest of the world. This has only gotten worse since the lockdowns and social distancing, but we can learn a lot from watching Jesus.

Obviously, he had his disciples. They were close and interesting for the time he traveled in the company and with the financial support of women. Jewish society wasn't always grace filled for women in that day, but the Messiah was one rabbi who embraced all people.

It has probably been pointed out too often, but our virtual connections through messaging, texting, and other electronic means have led to a large number of people who never developed the social skills they needed to be emotionally and mentally whole. And our entire society (and unfortunately too often, even God's people) are suffering as a result.

One of the big points of church that many miss is that it provides that "normal" for the human machine God designed. The Supreme Sovereign of the universe isn't *commanding* us to "go to church" as some cosmic game of Simon Says. He, out of his great love and longing for our well-being, instituted a family that we can all belong to. In this tight group of grace-filled people, we can receive the most valuable vitamin C—the C being *connection*.

Further, in a time when due to the *message of the medium,* when an increasing portion of our population desires to be famous, can we really say we are *following Christ* if that is our heart's desire? Sure, we can dress it up in spiritual-sounding terms—I want to speak, write, or perform *in order* to glorify God. Be careful with that. You may be fooling yourself. The desire to be famous, have a platform, or otherwise be highly thought of by others could also be just another symptom of being hacked. We see opinion leaders on social media, famous preachers, and other high-status individuals and are duped into believing that we need that same apparent success to feel better about ourselves. But of course we do dress it up in spiritualized language about serving God through our exalted and platformed self.

Are you willing to do the things that God has placed in front of you faithfully, even if no one knows about it? More on that later, in the chapter "Ditch the Cape."

No Books

Reading good books has been a casualty of the radio / television / electronic device revolution. It is a tragedy, and it harms us as a society. Allow me to explain.

Author Maryanne Wolf is, like me, a huge lover and advocate of reading. She writes wonderfully well. She has written a couple of excellent books on the problem of not reading and how much of our current electronic medium has contributed to this.

But in her book *Proust and the Squid: The Story and Science of the Reading Brain,* she makes a bold statement that I disagree with strongly:

> We were never born to read. Human beings invented reading only a few thousand years ago. And with this invention, we rearranged the very organization of our brain, which in turn expanded the ways in which we were able to think, which altered the intellectual evolution of our species.[57]

I applaud that she is true to her worldview, which is naturalistic and evolutionary. But being a person who now believes strongly in a *created world* and the biblical account of that creation, I contend the story is much different.

Our brains were intended to read and write from the get-go. It is part of the relational aspect mentioned earlier. Our Creator *is* the three-in-one all-time relational being, intimately communicating *always.* Much of Jesus's grief on the cross was due to the severance of the intimate bond with the Father and the Spirit in the moment he took on the gargantuan load of sin of the world.

But think back to the giving of the Ten Commandments. God *writes* with his own fingers on the tablets of stone. Our Creator preserved for his children the nature of his own heart—how we appropriately relate to him and to one another. He caused others, including Moses after the first tablets were thrown to the ground, to write as well.

Those he motivated preserved for us the precious stories of God interacting with his people, to correct, guide, and to save them.

No, I contend that we were wired to read and write—and for a very intimately important reason.

We need it.

I mentioned Dr. Robert Lustig earlier. He is by profession a pediatric endocrinologist with several decades of training and experience. Sitting down to read his book, which is an impressive and important work, I was struck by the importance of writing and reading in having the abundant life Jesus said he came to provide.

First of all, I do not have the time or the ability to become a pediatric endocrinologist. There is so much I could learn about the way in which companies trying to make money have learned to *hack* our endocrine and brain systems for profit.

And yet I do not have to become such a doctor to learn, for I can sit down with Dr. Lustig as he shares this important information that he is so passionate about. I sit down with him, and in a matter of hours, I am benefitting and gaining wisdom from all of his training. He is sharing through the written word the most important and cleanly distilled lessons of his decades of serving children and advocating for healthier lifestyles. All of this happens when I sit down and read his book. I do not see reading a book as *ingesting information* but as a life-transforming, wisdom-enhancing, mind-challenging, and intimate sharing opportunity.

One of the important factors Ms. Wolf and Mr. Nicholas Carr (quoted earlier) both mentioned is that, as they both adopted technology eagerly, when they returned to attempt reading, it had become difficult and unpleasant. Carr relates this in terms of the *neuroplasticity* of the brain—a remarkable design feature of our little noggin-resident gray matter. Neuroplasticity is the ability of our brain/mind to develop and expand to accommodate new abilities, even compensating in the event of a brain injury by moving a particular control area for a task to a different part of the brain.

But the problem with *not reading* is that a function not used tends to decline, and that brain space is used for something else that is regularly performed.

When I recommend to people that they should read more, I often get the "Well I tried, but I just don't get much out of it" excuse.

That's true. That's why you need to read more! The more you do it, the more you'll enjoy it.

Why so much talk about reading books in a section on your brain being hacked?

Because in order to *un-hack* your brain, you need to start putting down the devices and doughnuts and doing something that is good for you. Reading is essential!

Life is short, and just as I cannot go to med school for a number of reasons, I can read the works of doctors such as Dr. Lustig and benefit from his decades of experience and training. I can read the late-life lessons of famous politicians, soldiers, and everyday heroes and add their distilled life lessons to my own personal bag of hacks.

If you only live *your* life at the speed and ability you can without reading, you will only grow *at the speed of life or less.*

But to read voraciously and to read good literature—from a real book—that is the path to grow exponentially. It is truly a case of the proverbial standing on the shoulders of giants in order to grow in knowledge, wisdom, and ability beyond your years.

In your plan to un-hack your brain, reading should be the first thing you *plan* to do as an alternative to worshipping your electronic device or stuffing yourself with sugar.

Give all your effort to un-hacking yourself.

To the glory of God.

Dave out …

CHAPTER 5

Privileged and Oppressed Jesus

Everything can be taken from a man but one thing: the last of
the human freedoms—to choose one's attitude in any given
set of circumstances, to choose one's own way.
—Viktor Frankl

Feminism didn't just change American's understanding of sex
and gender roles. It changed the very meaning of life. It took
the spotlight off what matters—relationships and family—and put
it where it doesn't belong: on money, power, and fame.
—Suzanne Venker

Liberalism has also succeeded, tragically, in convincing blacks to see
themselves first and foremost as victims. Today there is no greater impediment to
black advancement than the self-pitying mindset that permeates black culture.
—Jason Riley

The Spirit of the Lord is upon me, because he has anointed me to
proclaim good news to the poor. He has sent me to proclaim liberty
to the captives and recovering of sight to the blind, to set at liberty
those who are oppressed, to proclaim the year of the Lord's favor.
—Isaiah the prophet

He was despised and rejected by men, a man of sorrows and
acquainted with grief; and as one from whom men hide their
faces he was despised, and we esteemed him not.
—Isaiah the prophet

I t was early summer in Tennessee, 2020. I was at home on a gorgeous morning.

It was in the middle of the ugly racial unrest going on in the wake of the death of George Floyd. I had been listening to a lot of people and reading books by a variety of authors on the topics of social justice and being black in America.

Today, my mind went on a journey of imagination I had never taken before. It was illuminating—challenging even.

What if I had been born me but black? What if everything were the same except that my family was blessed with the beautiful, dominant genetic trait for the expression of melanin?

Had I been black, growing up in a town that was 97 percent or so white, some things would have been very different. In the sixties and seventies, when I was a kid, there were still some serious vestiges of the old racism. It was small and rapidly disappearing, but it was still around. I would occasionally even hear someone my age saying horrible things about black people. I assumed that was the attitude they had caught from home, because it wasn't prevalent in our town.

I even remember sermons from the pulpit on whether or not black and white people should marry. The answer was it was okay scripturally, but it might be tough on the children, which upon reflection was entirely realistic at the time. On the other hand, women wearing pants to church was still pretty much a definite no-no!

But one thing that really grabbed me on my mental journey of the black me—if I had been *exactly me* in terms of my heart's desire in life to be a military and airline pilot, and being the grandson of a World War II veteran—was the absolute injustice of how black World War II veterans were treated differently *if* they survived the war, in one area in particular. This was an area that *could* have a multigenerational downstream impact.

It was regarding the GI Bill. The GI Bill was a benefit package of educational and business start-up help that proved transformational to many veterans' families. It was our nation's way of saying thank you to those who experienced some things in many cases that could never really be compensated for. The horrors that so many experienced would haunt and hurt them for the remainder of their lives.

Our black veterans fought the same war, paid the same price, and suffered the same—and the GI Bill was not given to those brave men. As a military veteran who fought in several wars, none of which were anywhere near the intensity and duration of World War II, it was just hard to conceive that anyone could have withheld this compensatory blessing to someone for something as insignificant as skin color. All soldiers bleed red. All soldiers' families cry the same tears.

Getting into flying was tough for me, but for many descendants of World War II, the GI Bill was transformative even to their grandchildren and beyond. Their grandfathers started businesses or new careers, enabling their families a leg up in their struggles as well. Because of the GI Bill, some grandsons of veterans who were my contemporaries had significantly more financial resources available due to the multigenerational heritage of success that had been passed along—likely the heritage of the GI Bill.

What if I had been the same young man looking longingly at the sky, dreaming of flight, but my family lacked the means to help me even get started toward this literally lofty goal—just because of my grandfather's genetic melanin level?

I would have to wonder how things would have differed for black me if my grandfather had been offered the same treatment for the same sacrifice. What was done was grossly unjust. It pains me to think of the mindset present in someone's heart to even consider such a thing as a formal government (and therefore, societal) policy. It was coldhearted and inhumane.

It was a sad thought that day—but there's more to it. We'll come back to my grandfather and my venture into aviation a bit later. It is instructive as to the true nature of life *and* opportunity. It is also helpful in unpacking the issue of *equity* that is so often brought up today. But for now, how about we investigate God's view on injustice.

Jesus Talking to a Dog's Dog

The scriptures are full of passages expressing God's love for *all people*. He does not play favorites. Further, in the creation account, each and every person is made as an *image bearer* of God—we all have inestimable inherent worth in the eyes of God. To treat someone badly because of their appearance (the sum total of the differences between any discernable visible difference between any people on earth is *nothing but appearance*) is to insult God himself—something called *blasphemy*. It is, along with idolatry (which to consider oneself superior due to some external characteristic would make one an idolatrous blasphemer), one of the worst sins—for far from just disobeying God, one is also attacking his person and his work!

The one story that soundly demonstrates what our attitude toward the ideology of *social justice* should be is from the story of Jesus and his encounter with the woman at the well we mentioned in the last chapter. It is found in John, chapter 4, but the following is a quick analysis of it.

Jesus needs to travel to a certain place, and his disciples (learners) are with him. He is Jewish, as are his followers to this point. Some have called the Jews a "race" (most notably, Adolf Hitler), but this is not true. Race is a creation of man. The current concept of race is a modification of a concept that we inherited from Charles Darwin and his cronies—and it is a hideous thing.

His concept was that we evolved from lower species and that *some* of us were further along the evolutionary pathway (i.e., superior) to others. He saw black people, in particular, as more *apelike* and thus of a lower refinement and worth than white people. He did not restrict his idolatrous and blasphemous hubris just to blacks, but dark-skinned people have always bore the brunt of the racial-minded and population control crowds as being "less than." Notice where most Planned Parenthood clinics are located. There is a tragic agenda with these organizations.

Jews are not a *race*; they are just a *family*. They are the descendants of Jacob and his twelve sons. There is nothing significant about them genetically, any more than any other people group.

Back to Jesus, his Jewish (family) followers, and their journey. They were leaving Judea and going to Galilee. If you look on the map, the most direct route is through Samaria. There is a valley through the mountains, and Samaria is along that path.

But any self-respecting Jew would not soil their feet with the dirt of Samaria, nor would the Samaritans necessarily treat a Jew who took the easier path very kindly. The Jews and Samaritans were family, but the Jews considered their brothers and sisters to have been "tainted" and thus "less than" through intermarrying during a period when the land of Israel had been occupied by a foreign power. There had been much animus, mistreatment, and even violence between the two people groups—even though they were related. There was truly no significant difference between them—just as there are no meaningful differences between anyone on earth today. Men and women have some differences, and we praise God for that. But those differences are pretty much the same across what is called "races" of people.

Wouldn't you know it. Jesus does what no self-respecting rabbi would have done. He goes straight into Samaria. People would talk.

They stop at a well near the town of Sychar, and Jesus sends his followers into town to get food. I personally believe that he knew who was coming to the well and that he needed to be one-on-one with someone because of what many today would erroneously call "the racial tensions."

Anyway, a woman does come to the well in the middle of the day after the disciples left. The timing is probably because she is disliked and shunned by the other men and women of Samaria. Hauling water was hard work, best done in the cool of the day. But at the best time of day, the other women of the community would have been there. This woman who Jesus meets is possibly trying to avoid others due to shame or rejection.

You see, the Jews would often call Samaritans "dogs," and this was not in the sense of a fuzzy and loved house pet. It would be the same as a call of "cracker," "gook," or "nigger" in our nation's recent past.

This woman was the dog of the dogs. Women did not generally have high standing in either Samaritan or Jewish society, but this woman (as we discover from the words of Jesus) has been married five times and is currently shacking up with some other man— something sinful and frowned upon in both societies of the day.

In terms of our current philosophy of placing people in identity groups in order to justify mistreatment and the withholding of good things from them (i.e., "social justice" or "intersectionality"), this woman of Samaria has lost the lottery in her day. She belongs not only to the identity group "Samaritan" but also "dog," "woman," "divorcee," and "slut." She has been placed in a seriously bad intersection of identity.

While the disciples and even the everyday "good" people of Samaria may not have thought in feminist intersectional terms, this is where she would have been pigeonholed to the self-respecting members of both groups. She was guilty by classification of being Samaritan and a woman. She was guilty personally of shacking up. The reasons for her divorces are not listed, but in the case of a woman, that identity meant that you were worth less anyway.

Not that you were worth much to begin with.

So how does Jesus handle her *identity* as a rising rabbi who is just beginning to get notoriety?

Simple. He treated her with the grace, mercy, and dignity that every single human being should be treated with. She was, in spite of the challenges and perhaps some failures she had experienced, a beloved image bearer of our magnificent God—and therefore she was magnificent and in need of love.

She bore no responsibility before this Jewish man for the previous Samaritan desecration of the temple in Jerusalem. She bore no censure for being what she was created as by our mutual loving creator—a bearer and nurturer of life, a woman. She was a sinner in need of grace, and Jesus extended that grace by talking to her (which surprised her greatly) as a brother would to a sister—for we are all of the same family, really.

She also was a person just like you and me (at least I can vouch for me), who in her fleshly weakness had made some decisions that seemed to offer comfort but were at odds with the purity of God. She needed to repent, to turn away from those things that God tells us are sin. Sins are those things that violate the purity and person of who God is. And pretty much universally, sin is also something that harms us as well; God's commandments are given for our own good.

Jesus didn't sugarcoat this reality, nor did he excuse her by rationalizing that this was just the way she was born. "Hey, sweetie, God didn't make you to stay married, so in your case, shacking up is the only way to go," was not advice given by our Lord. He just stated where she was and left it there for her to deal with as she was able.

There is no room in the life and teaching of Jesus for identity mistreatment, or *intersectionality / critical race theory* in the modern vernacular. The categories that are used today are just as contrived and meaningless as those in the day of Jesus. A Samaritan, dog, Jew, Scythian, or tax collector all were treated by Jesus with the dignity, love, and respect due to someone made in the image of God.

Jesus's actions were harsh and direct with those who were religiously presumptuous (the Pharisees, for example) or those who approached him in pretense (the Syro-Phoenician woman[58]) in an apparent attempt to get their attention and call them off their pretense. If they responded repentantly, he then treated them with grace, love, and dignity.

If Jesus's behavior is not enough to call us away from these atrocious ideologies of social justice and intersectionality, then shouldn't the legacy of them be? In the twentieth century alone, more than two hundred million people died as the result of being pegged into various identities for *correction*—Jew, bourgeois, Gypsy, black, and the list goes on. How many more tens of millions of innocent people must die before we learn to treat people in the way that Jesus demonstrated?

Showing favoritism to anyone because of something they have no control over (skin color and gender) and punishing/withholding grace from others for the same reason is sin and is truly oppressive.

It is nothing new, just repackaged in new "progressive" terms— but it is the same path followed by Communists in Russia, China, and Cambodia that led to mass graves and the deaths of tens of millions.

It was the same path chosen by Adolf Hitler with the backing of "science" to exterminate Jews, blacks, and Gypsies.

No follower of God can embrace this.

Ever.

Past Injustices

No doubt, going back to the *black me*, if my family had been the victims of past systemic racism (through denial of the GI Bill or other forms that happened in the past), there could be (and are at times) downstream effects of that. So how do we correct those past injustices?

During all of my adult life, this correction was attempted through preferential hiring and promotion practices. These had differing names or at times were kept silent, but it was well known that if you were black or a woman, you could just about name your ticket in military or commercial aviation. The same was true in higher education. Colleges and scholarships were far more accessible if your met certain minority or gender criteria.

My military unit was part of the Air National Guard system, so you could be in the military *and* get hired and work elsewhere. Most of our pilots (myself included) were shooting for the major airlines. The airlines had always required a lot of turbine (jet engine or jet-prop) experience, along with a substantial amount of pilot-in-command experience (think captain of a large aircraft or single-seat fighter-type flying) in order to get hired.

One of my military friends got hired at a major airline with pretty much *none* of those things. When he told me his good news about the new job, he was a bit defensive right off the bat. "I got hired because I typed my application and had the right number of recommendations."

"No. You're black," I replied.

"No, no, really, they like it when you type your application and have three recommendations," he protested.

"Hey, you're black, and I'm happy for you. If they were looking for middle-aged guys with receding hairlines, I'd get in line for the job. I'd just be honest about why I was hired," I answered.

Now here's the thing. Every wannabe pilot was typing their applications and getting three recommendations; that gouge on that airline was well known. His defense was spurious.

But this airline had years before gotten in trouble for its allegations of unfair hiring practices. They had lowered their hiring standards in order to get more women and minorities on board. I don't suppose they felt they had a choice, since the federal government was the one threatening them if they didn't meet certain quotas.

But you should ask, why did the airlines *all* have such high standards for jet time and pilot-in-command time to begin with? Was it some ploy to keep *undesirable* minorities and women out of the cockpit? Or were they looking for mature aviators with a significant history of successfully flying in order to keep the traveling public safe?

I have asked a few social justice believers—when you put your family on an airliner, which do you value more? A racially and gender-balanced cockpit or staying alive?

Everyone wants to stay alive. No one gives a flip about the politics of the cockpit. Nor should they. We want someone who is competent, experienced, professional, and able to handle any challenges or emergencies that arise.

People just want good pilots.

They don't care if she's black, green, white, or if she's not a she. Everyone has a shared goal of staying alive.

They just don't want that thin-skinned aluminum tube moving through the air at 600 mph to crash into the ground with their precious little pink, crunchy bodies strapped inside. That's perfectly understandable, and it indicates this—human life is precious, and there is *no place* for politically and ideologically motivated hiring into critical careers fields.

We are *not* correcting for past injustices by lowering the hiring standards for airline pilots, doctors, nurses, police officers, or anyone else; we are just being *unjust*. We may be causing the deaths of many while treating others with a lack of dignity.

Plus, we need to understand that God *is* justice. True justice flows from who he is in his perfect heart. If we are being just, then we are treating our fellow man in a way that is resonating with the truth of who God is.

Scripture makes it abundantly clear that penalizing someone for something they did not do is *ungodly*:

> The word of the Lord came to me: "What do you mean by repeating this proverb concerning the land of Israel, 'The fathers have eaten sour grapes, and the children's teeth are set on edge?' As I live, declares the Lord God, this proverb shall no more be used by you in Israel. Behold, all souls are mine; the soul of the father as well as the soul of the son is mine; the soul who sins shall die."[59]

In God's heart, it is dead wrong to punish a child for the sins of the father. It is clearly a sin to punish someone for their skin color, gender, or other trait they have no control over. Such injustice is pure evil, and as one would expect, much of the current talk about white privilege, social justice, and gender disparities are based upon lies, myths, and strongly held societal delusions.

I have a dear friend who is black and a very honest talker. He says what's on his mind. One day he told me over lunch, "I wish I was white."

"I wish I was black," I retorted.

"What? Why would you want that?" he asked incredulously.

"First of all, I'd have that great tan like you have instead of this pasty white skin with moles and freckles. Second, I would have gotten an airline job at least a decade earlier, it would have been easier, and I would have made millions more in career earnings!" I answered cheerfully.

It was all true. In fact, when I talk with my social justice–advocating friends, I always ask a specific question that does have a specific answer: "Give me an example of ongoing systemic racism."

It is always met with an awkward pause, then some discussion on past red-lining of certain urban areas (basically businesses withholding financing for homes/businesses based upon the ethnic makeup of an area, which did happen in the past), voting restrictions (those happened also in the past), and the like. But nothing ongoing. But there is ongoing racial *and* gender-based discrimination.

It is in plain sight.

It is on every job, college, and financial aid application.

It is labeled with checkboxes as "sex" or "gender" and "race."

As authors Heather McDonald and Candace Owen noted in one interview, the one area of truly systemic discrimination that still remains in America is against the white male. Ms. Owens, who is black and married to a white man, humorously noted that while she and her husband were not planning on raising any children of theirs as any "race" other than human, when it came time to apply for college admission or financial aid, then their kids were definitely *black* or *African American*. Because that was (at the time of the interview) the most privileged and most likely to be selected identity group in America.

But is it *just* to penalize someone for something they didn't do, or for being in an arbitrarily defined identity group that they have no control over belonging to?

Absolutely not. It is unjust, at least from the perspective of our Creator.

His perspective is the only one that matters, by the way.

So how does this work out regarding past injustices?

I finished my military career in 2007 and am nearing the end of my airline career. As mentioned earlier, had I been black or female, or the holy grail of all privilege, a black female, my career trajectory would have been exponentially faster and more lucrative. I lost, literally, millions of dollars of career earnings because of my choosing to be white and male.

Oh, by the way, I *didn't* choose those.

I was discriminated against for thirty-plus years, and my family was denied the benefits that would have accrued had I been black or female or, best of all, both.

Should we penalize blacks, females, and especially black females to correct for this injustice? Should a thirty-year-old have to give up a portion of her income (along with others of the currently chosen privileged classes) because of the injustices leveled against me?

Of course not. That, too, would be unjust.

There is no standard of true justice in which someone is penalized for something they did not do, nor should anyone be penalized for their skin color, ear shape, or gender—all things that have zero significance in life and that are genetic traits we do not get to choose.

What is to be done to restore my equity with a similar-aged black male or female airline pilot who was given privilege in hiring and thus did much better than me?

The only just way of correcting a past injustice is to stop the *present* injustice.

The reality of life is that sometimes people are ugly in their actions, and others suffer as a result. At some point, the ugliness needs to be stopped, and we all need to learn from the injustice—and proceed with compassion and love toward our fellow image bearers of our beautiful God. I know, and this is one of the reasons why I have joy in my life, that sometimes life is *not* fair. I was on the wrong side of the *oppression Olympics* (a fun name given to the feminist concept of *intersectionality*), and there was not really anything to be done about it at the time. The political and therefore the justice climate was not favorable (things were unjust). My prayer is that at some point we will start treating people according to their character and not according to the color of their skin or their gender (biological sex, to be clear).

That last statement—sound familiar? It is a paraphrase of Dr. Martin Luther King Jr. and his "I Have a Dream" speech. In it, not only did he *dream* of people being judged by the content of their character—but something even grander, grace filled, and godly.

He dared to dream of a time when someone would look out on a playground of children and see *children*. Not black, white, yellow, or red children—just precious human souls created beautifully in the image of their Creator God.

Now you realize that, according to the dictates of advocates of critical race theory and intersectionality, that makes Dr. King a *white racist oppressor*. Because under those views, one must look on the playground and see white male heteronormative oppressors cursed with ableism, and the rest of the children are victims, totally at the mercy of their powerful three-year-old white male oppressors—that is, of course, unless the messianic and benevolent government steps in to save the poor, helpless victims and endow them with power.

Of course, if the three-year-old white boy *identifies* as a black female lesbian transgender, then perhaps he might have a few intersections of goodness, but probably not enough to overcome the dreaded and deadly whiteness and toxic masculinity of this sweet-looking but nefarious toddler.

Am I taking this too far? That is the accusation I receive by advocates of the hateful doctrines of social justice. But I say no. The pathway to genocide and stacks of cold, emaciated bodies is paved with these old but renamed concepts of artificial identity injustice.

We need to stop the seesaw cycle of vengeance before it results in the old human traditions of mass graves and truly heinous suffering. Far too often, in the former USSR, in Nazi Germany, Communist China, and Cambodia, the people doing the torture and killing were the neighbors of the victims (as mentioned earlier). They had been deluded into believing what they were doing was for the betterment of society and that it was necessary.

We may say that "Hitler killed six million Jews," and there is truth to that, but the gritty reality is that it was the fellow citizens of the Jews who enabled and even accomplished the killing.

We humans have pretty much an unlimited ability to delude ourselves and rationalize our hatefulness. Back to our earlier quote from the writings of Ezekiel, there was an interesting idea that had arisen in Israel, and the Lord God himself, of course, was listening and commented on it.

The idea was summarized by this statement: "The way of the Lord is not just."[60]

Why would they say such a thing? It is tantamount to saying, "God is dead." Or perhaps, "God is evil and wrong."

Here's the deal. Let's see if this resonates with any current philosophies about justice:

> Yet you say, "Why should not the son suffer for the iniquity of the father?"[61]

Understand this is God himself quoting to Ezekiel what the people of Israel have been saying. Our Father hears us, and that should make us think deeply and critically about what it is we are saying. For in this instance, he heard what was being said and was quick to point out that the behavior of the Jewish people was unacceptable.

When any one of God's creatures (that'd be everyone) states that it is okay to withhold the good things of life or to treat someone poorly because of the identity group we (or someone else) has placed them in, that is a direct violation of the justice and mercy of God.

One of the Many Reasons I Believe

The Bible is gritty and real. It describes all the foulness and pure hatred of the selfish human heart in detail. It presents no perfect world possibilities on this side of heaven. Humankind will never be perfected and living in perfect harmony. The Bible never promises a utopian state if it is followed perfectly, because it admits that because of the sinful nature (the flesh), none of us will be able to keep it perfectly—thus we have the need of grace.

This is just another of the many reasons I believe the Word to be true. It presents life on earth as it consistently is.

God *could* in theory (but because of his great love, could not) have made us as little automatic robots who had no choice but to obey him and be nice.

It would have been pointless and a gruelingly meaningless existence. Therefore, a loving and just God *could not* have created us this way.

God's desire has always been for a loving relationship with his creatures, not slavery.

To experience true love, of the agape type, requires liberty and freedom to choose one's response to our Creator and this life he has gifted to us.

Humans, given this liberty, frequently chose not to trust their maker and instead created their own path of faux wisdom.

In the wake of humanity's disobedience and arrogance, humans suffer and die by the tens of millions.

We had more than a century of the mistreatment of many people groups in America—and now with critical race theory and intersectionality, many are advocating that we accelerate mistreatment once again. Their lack of understanding of history, truth, and of God himself is leading our nation (and others) down the path of atrocities and mass graves.

Or as it is popularly called, *social justice.* Sounds nice, eh? What would our Creator say to it?

> Woe to those who call evil good and good evil, who put darkness for light and light for darkness, who put bitter for sweet and sweet for bitter! Woe to those who are wise in their own eyes, and shrewd in their own sight.[62]

If the God who gave you life is pronouncing "woe" upon you now, you must repent. Social justice, the concept of white privilege, critical race theory, intersectionality, microaggression, and all other such concepts are a violation of the purity and beauty of the heart of the Sovereign Lord of the universe.

Repent.

The Reality of My Grandpa

I said we'd get back to this instructive lesson about my World War II navy veteran grandfather.

He was *not* black, and thus he was given the opportunity of the GI Bill. What difference did the equity of that opportunity among nonblack veterans make in my family's life?

None whatsoever.

You can try to *give* equity. It does not work.

The reason my family was poorer than some is because of choices made by my family.

First of all, my grandfather, upon returning home from the war, didn't want to go to school to enhance his education or abilities. Nor

71

did he have a desire to start a business. As far as I know, he never touched his GI Bill.

He was happy, by all accounts, to return to his old, unsophisticated but connected way of life. He loved being a firefighter. He went back to that.

He also loved making things with his hands. He worked in a tin shop, making things out of metal. It wasn't very lucrative or admired work, but he found satisfaction in it.

He was very tall in that generation, and his nickname from the navy was "Tiny." A lot of people still called him that when he got home. But he was known for his big heart.

He loved taking his sons out for breakfast, talking with his friends, and being with family. He was one of those veterans who, upon his return home, rarely talked about the war.

His life demonstrates just one way in which *equity* (equal possessions, wealth, or social status) just does not happen.

My grandfather was happy where he was before the war, just living in a small community and being with friends and family, contributing through work to his society. There is nothing wrong with that.

Our country offered him *more* through the GI Bill, and he politely declined. He didn't want more.

He just desired to go back to the comfortable life he had before the war—as much as possible. While some might condemn his lack of ambition, I admire him for his simple love of life. Maybe things would have been easier for me if he had used his GI Bill and started a huge business, but then again, I probably wouldn't have been born.

You can't *give* equity, because some people do not or will not use the things you have taken from others in the same way. Equal results will never happen. Equal opportunity to strive or not strive is justice.

My Other Relatives and Jesus

My grandfather's sons were some of the most intelligent and funny guys I've ever known. All three of these guys could regularly make me laugh so hard that I would hurt.

They had enormous potential to succeed spectacularly, to have lots of wealth, possessions, and status.

My dad had some bouts of success and social status, but for the most part, he frittered away his money on women, drugs, alcohol, and poor life decisions. He made the kind of decisions that lead to anyone not doing well in life and paid the predictable heavy price.

My uncles, his two brothers, lived right around or well below poverty level all their lives. They, too, were addled by the consequences of specific behavioral and belief system choices that keep people poor, unhealthy, and unsuccessful. Both committed suicide later in life.

These three brothers were not successful and are a good demonstration of the problem that claiming a lack of home ownership, money, status, or success are something that can be corrected through taking from others and giving to those who are perceived to be behind.

My grandfather was content where he was. He was offered a program (the GI Bill) that *could* have changed the success trajectory of him and all those who followed him. But he was *content*. I respect that.

My dad and his brothers, on the other hand, consistently made choices (sex outside of marriage, alcohol use to assuage pain, drug use, a general lack of discipline, low educational level by choice/laziness) that for nearly anyone leads to a life of misery. The apparent lack of equity was *not* the result of discrimination of any sort. It was just the natural consequence of the choices they made in the way they lived.

They picked up one end of a stick, and the other end came with it.

73

My dad and his two brothers demonstrate the truth of a curious thing Jesus said: "For you always have the poor with you."[63]

Sometimes people are poor because of oppression.

Sometimes that oppression is what was demonstrated by my dad and his uncles—self-oppression.

It is a major problem in the black community today.

The Census Says …

In the process of writing this chapter, my wife asked for some help on census data for the area in which I lived. She had started a new job in adult education and needed the data. What I stumbled upon in the research was very telling.

While Ibram X. Kendi may claim that it is the white people who are systemically privileged and that is why black people are so often living in poverty, the data shows something significant about the untruth of his claim.

In Dickson County, Hispanics are more minority than blacks. Yet they have the lowest poverty rates of any artificial categories of people in the county, including whites.

What a privileged group of oppressors these Hispanics are, no?

Of course, if your community is like mine, you know that many of these Hispanics are first- or second-generation citizens (or in some cases are here illegally). Why is their poverty rate so much lower?

The Hispanic folks work hard. A lot of the construction/home-improvement companies use almost exclusively such people. This minority often start their own businesses—but whatever the case, I am always impressed by their work ethic. They bust it all day long. They bring their lunch in a sack and eat quickly in the yard. Hot or cold, wet or dry—they work all day and do excellent work.

They are also generally devoted Christians (a strong Catholic tradition, often), are very devoted to their families, and they live very frugally. They live their faith—they value getting married instead of shacking up.

In other words, they choose to engage in the known behaviors that produce success, wealth, and overall well-being in all of humanity.

Author Thomas Sowell pointed out in his excellent work, *Black Rednecks and White Liberals*,[64] that southern whites who adopted certain values suffered nearly universal poverty, poor health, and misery:

> The cultural values and social patterns among Southern whites included an aversion to work, proneness to violence, neglect of education, sexual promiscuity, improvidence, drunkenness, lack of entrepreneurship, reckless searches for excitement, lively music and dance, and a style of religious oratory marked by strident rhetoric, unbridled emotions, and flamboyant imagery. This oratorical style carried over into the political oratory of the region in both the Jim Crow era and the civil rights era, and has continued on into our own times among black politicians, preachers, and activists today. Touchy pride, vanity, and boastful self-dramatization were also part of this redneck culture among people from regions of Britain "where the civilization was the least developed.[65]

Sowell goes into great detail of the chosen attitudes and lifestyles that produced what is still known in the South as the *redneck* or even *white trash* (my words; I grew up and still live in the South, where this is evident) cultural tradition.

It is stunningly sad to this day to see people suffering poverty, poor health, and violence and passing this on to their progeny writ large, but as Sowell points out, the tragic results of redneck living are just the predictable consequences of their societally valued choices. Those very choices, when made by anyone, regardless of the genetic

STEPHEN K. MOORE

repression or dominant expression of melanin (i.e., skin color), produce the same tragic results.

Sowell pointedly sums up this truth:

> The point here is that cultural differences led to striking socioeconomic differences among blacks, as they did among whites. In both races, those who lived within the redneck culture lagged far behind those who did not.[66]

In other words, the worst oppression an individual goes through in western society is *self-oppression*. Choosing to go along with a life of ease, partying, faux glamour, alcohol, drugs, easy unmarried sex, and marginal literacy produces a nearly guaranteed result—a life of poverty and misery.

Victim Blaming?

Am I engaging in the forbidden sin of victim blaming? Let's talk.

It was fun going through the training for the marriage and family therapy program at a liberal Jewish university.

On the one hand, a veritable avalanche of solid research data and a rich heritage of Jewish thinkers continually pounded home the truth that the consistently most well-adjusted and resilient people *take responsibility for their choices.* To see oneself as a victim is the surest and quickest route to misery and failure.

In my coursework, I would often counter the contentions of some of the professors and students advocating for the victim/oppressor paradigm by quoting Holocaust survivor Viktor Frankl:

> Everything can be taken from a man but one thing: the last of the human freedoms—to choose one's attitude in any given set of circumstances, to choose one's own way.[67]

I got many responses typified by the statement, "Oh, I love Viktor Frankl!" But of course, my thought was, *What do you mean by love?* Since it seemed everyone had nothing for contempt for one of the most important lessons learned from the death of six million Jews. How can you throw away that lesson for the popularity of advocating that the last of the human freedoms was *your choosing* to blame others for your situation?

His quote above is preceded by a vital discussion and questioning of the nature of human life under the horrible conditions of the Nazi prison camps:

> In attempting this psychological presentation and a psychopathological explanation of the typical characteristics of a concentration camp inmate, I may give the impression that the human being is completely and unavoidably influenced by his surroundings. (In this case the surroundings being the unique structure of camp life, which forced the prisoner to conform his conduct to a certain forced pattern). But what about human liberty? Is there no spiritual freedom in regard to behavior and reaction to any given surroundings? Is that theory true which would have us believe that man is no more than a product of many conditional and environmental factors—be they of a biological, psychological or sociological nature? Is man but an accidental product of these? Most important, do the prisoners' reactions to the singular world of the concentration camp prove that man cannot escape the influences of his surroundings? Does man have no choice of actions in the face of such circumstances?
>
> We can answer these questions from experience as well as on principle. The experiences of camp life

show that man does have a choice of action. There were enough examples, often of a heroic nature, which proved that apathy could be overcome, irritability suppressed. Man can preserve a vestige of spiritual freedom, of independence of mind, even in such terrible conditions of psychic and physical stress.

We who lived in concentration camps can remember the men who walked through the huts comforting others, giving away their last piece of bread. They may have been few in number, but they offer sufficient proof that *everything can be taken from a man but one thing: the last of the human freedoms—to choose one's attitude in any given set of circumstances, to choose one's own way.*[68]

The current ideology of critical race theory and intersectionality is a cruel mockery of the suffering and death of millions of fellow human beings in the Holocaust and in the Communist/socialist experiments in the last century. It is a retrograde choice to embrace the long march to mass graves based upon hatred, ignorance, and envy.

What's Your Locus?

One of the most consistent findings in psychology over the last century is that the happiest of people have a certain view regarding who is in control of their lives.

To cut to the chase, those who see themselves as victims do not do well in life. That is called an *external locus of control.* This is a view of life that sees life as something that happens to you—and either you are dealt a good hand or a bad one.

People with an external locus are universally miserable, poor, and angry. They often desire power over others in order to extract vengeance and live off the sweat of the brows of others.

At the other extreme is the *internal locus of control*—which is the view that life is in your hands. This is a healthier and more successful view. But there is a third view, which is biblical and even better in terms of the joy you experience in life:

> Thus, in reference to locus of control, the optimal level of happiness is achieved by a balanced locus of control expectancy, which is a combination of internal and external locus of control expectancy, known also as shared responsibility, dual control, or bi-local expectancy. This highlights the importance of recognizing and individual's own ability to influence his/her life and the environment, while having regard for the fact that certain aspects may be uncontrollable by the individual and may be impacted by chance or powerful others.[69]

This is what bi-local expectancy looked like in my life as a white male in military and commercial aviation.

There was a systemic bias against white males my entire career. There was a huge push to hire minority and female pilots. The standards were lowered for *that identity group* to attempt to achieve some significant participation in the aviation workforce (i.e., "equity"). You could actually make the case that the standards were nearly eliminated.

At air force pilot training, it was easy to *wash out,* to be kicked out of the yearlong primary training program.

Unless you were a minority or female.

In my class, one of my friends was a female wannabe military pilot. She wanted to fly so badly she could taste it. She was determined not to fail. But she was struggling.

When you had trouble in pilot training, if you failed a certain number of flights, you would go to what was called a Flight Evaluation Board (FEB). It was understood, if you were a white male, that if you failed your last flight on a Friday and they scheduled your FEB for Monday, you could start packing up your goods for the move on Saturday. The FEB was just a formality, for you were *gone*.

You would show up before a panel of commanders and instructors, and they would present your history in the program. Then you would be allowed to present your case as to why you should remain in the program. Then they would say, "Thank you for your input," and tell you to go away. You were done.

Unless you were female or a minority or both.

My female comrade made it to her *third* FEB before she was eliminated.

Was it fair to the rest of us that a different standard was applied to women or minorities but not us?

No.

Was it oppressive?

I guess.

But back to the bi-local expectation of control. Could I do anything about it?

Realistically, there was nothing I could have done that would have been successful in the political justice climate at the time. A lawsuit would have likely been laughed out of court. I would have been called a *misogynistic, privileged, patriarchal bigot* for even bringing it up. I might have even been called out for my greatest sin, that of being white. I'm not sure why I chose to be a white male sometimes.

I'm okay with all of that. As a white male, I have been denigrated, humiliated, and made fun of all my life. No worries. It's just the way life has been all my life.

It was also a situation I had no control over. And frankly, I didn't want to be patronized in order to get my air force wings. I wanted to *exceed* the standards, not be given a pass.

Aviation *had* high standards because it is a profession of a daily life-and-death nature. There is no room for changing the standards in order to achieve equality of results. The aviation environment does not give one iota of respect to your skin color or gender. It is an equal opportunity killer.

I didn't want a concession for any inability I might possess. I wanted to be the best pilot that I could be or be shown the respect and dignity to be told that I shouldn't be in the profession.

As to the unfairness in future hiring and opportunities, there was really nothing to be done to change that. What I could do was choose my attitude and let the God of Creation direct my path through an unfair situation. I would choose to love others, even if they were theoretically in the identity group that was given a free pass. Were they my oppressors? No, not at all. They just sort of benefitted from the misguided and evil actions of the actual oppressors.

Because, as I honestly shared earlier, I would have accepted the free pass into the airlines for a middle-aged white guy with a receding hairline in my thirties if it had been offered. But I didn't want to be given a pass on the skills needed to be the best pilot I could possibly be—to avoid an untimely and stupid death (and possibly the death of many others riding in my aircraft).

My path to a successful military and airline career was harder for me than it would have been if I had been black or female. For that, I am thankful. Everything worth doing is hard, and I have always found that in the struggle, I appreciated every gain along the way so much more because of the struggle.

In fact, many of my friends who had moneyed families or racial/gender privilege (i.e., black or female) advanced rapidly past me, but with so many of those I was able to stay in touch with, they had nowhere near the level of joy or satisfaction with their careers that I did.

That which is easily obtained is lightly esteemed.

The Biblical Drill Down on Social Justice Theories

My prayer is that if you have been an advocate for current social justice theories, our Lord has touched your heart and mind in the same way he did mine.

The theories, whether critical race or intersectionality, are emotion-driven versions of the old Marxist ploy of hatred and envy toward arbitrarily chosen identity groups that ignore the image of God, individual worth, and loveliness of every creature God created.

Social justice is absolutely unjust and an affront to our mutual, loving Creator.

In our virtually connected but lonelier than ever world, the social justice cause allows a person to feel virtuous while embracing evil. By embracing this ideology, you get little dopamine strokes online while sitting on your butt doing nothing. Social justice causes are a manipulation of the desire born of the image of God within to do good to all. But instead of doing good, we simply inflate our public image by embracing the sin of punishing someone for something they did not do, based upon an arbitrary assignment of their *identity* that has no validity with God himself.

The true cause of justice can be embraced and enacted upon by the following, what Yeshua the Messiah identified as the two most important commands from the covenant with Israel:

> The most important is, "Hear, O Israel: The Lord our God, the Lord is one. And you shall love the Lord your God with all your heart and with all your soul and with all your mind and with all your strength." The second is this: "You shall love your neighbor as yourself." There is no commandment greater than these.[70]

Just to be clear, this *is* the solution to injustice and oppression. And to make very clear in our current electronically connected but actually disconnected from love generations, to *love* your neighbor involves *knowing* them and *doing* for them.

Not just posting or standing in a protest line.

Jesus walked straight into Samaria, the no-Jews land, and met with the dog's dog. He spent days with the marginalized people of Sychar, Samaria. He and the identity-crippled, marginalized dog's dog of a woman started a spiritual revolution of love there.

Victims can't do that.

People walking in the Spirit and love of God can.

Love, actually.

It's that simple, but you have to break away from your phone and actually talk to someone. You actually have to *love,* not just type with your thumbs and declare yourself virtuous and good.

Imagine that.

Pruning the Root of Bitterness

Back in the nineties, there was a black brother in Christ I knew as "Brother Onnie." He organized some men's prayer gatherings during that time, and he said something prior to one of the prayer times that was challenging to me: "I know we have many black and white brothers here, and there is much hurt between us. There is much to forgive, but we must forgive."

Given what we have already spoken of in terms of biblical truth, this was not technically true. There was likely no basis for hurt and hard feelings in this group if we looked at the sin of each man toward one another.

At the same time, there was a large number of black brothers who had been raised with an awareness of the past mistreatment of their families based upon skin color—usually at the hands of someone with white skin color.

Further, the dominant story of our culture was one of victimization, marginalization, and the "my people were hurt by your people" messages.

One way or another, there was hurt and anger. There was guilt and sorrow on the part of many if not all of the white brothers, even though none of them personally had anything to do with what had happened.

In doing marriage counseling and teaching, I always stress that if your marriage partner perceives there is a problem, then you have a problem. One person in the relationship assigned blame or motives against the other wrongly, and while the other person may be innocent, the fact that the perception is there is still a problem that needs to be dealt with.

The simple fact is that in this actually insignificant difference in the genetic expression or repression of melanin in our skin, for a number of reasons, there is much anger, bitterness, confusion, and guilt to be dealt with.

The writer of the book of Hebrews goes into a discussion of the discipline of the Lord, noting,

> My son, do not regard lightly the discipline of the
> Lord, nor be weary when reproved by him. For the
> Lord disciplines the one he loves, and chastises very
> son whom he receives.[71]

This truth has many applications, but think about this *racial* and *oppression* issue we have been discussing.

For all of my life, I had heard messages regarding the white oppression of blacks. It is a bitter legacy that is hard to grasp in our time. Why, or even *how,* could someone look at a fellow creature of God and see anything but beauty and worth?

The history of our world is replete, unfortunately, with the stories of man's cruelty to his fellow man, of men mistreating women, of women abusing men, of parents neglecting children, of murder and exploitation.

It creates anger in our souls and a recognition that it never should have happened—nor should it ever happen again.

But it has, and it will.

Many of the potential downstream effects we witness today were originated by persons long gone.

What do we do with our anger, guilt, and desire for righteousness? The writer of Hebrews anticipated our plight:

> Therefore lift your drooping hands and strengthen your weak knees, and make straight paths for your feet, so that what is lame may not be put out of joint but rather be healed. Strive for peace with everyone, and for the holiness without which no one will see the Lord. See to it that no one fails to obtain the grace of God; that no root of bitterness springs up and causes trouble, and by it many become defiled.[72]

The reality of life on earth is that it is filled with challenging and often ugly situations that leave us feeling angry, guilty, or sad.

The Lord permits, and perhaps in some cases even directs, us into events that challenge us—for the purpose of not leaving us where we are. He wants us to grow, to experience the abundance of a holy life lived in wisdom.

What can we do to prevent this root of bitterness regarding past injustices based upon ignorance from festering into a future of violence and further sin?

From the passage above, several points are made:

1. *Seek the grace of God.* I really find Jesus to be the hardest example to beat in terms of dealing with actual oppression.

He was truly God, and he condescended to come to earth to be born as a human child, with all the constraints and discomfort that entailed. He came to help all humanity and yet found himself continually mistreated and opposed at every turn.

He endured it, he prayed for his enemies, and he showed us the path to peace.

That path is Jesus himself.

Grace is costly to the one who gives it. Go in the imagination our Creator has endowed us with and look at the Messiah on the cross. Giving grace is at times immensely costly; it requires us to give up our demand for immediate fairness and trust that God is sovereign and will work all things together for good.

2. *Strive for peace with everyone.* I have made a strong case against social justice and its various components, but I love my friends who advocate for it. They have good hearts—they desire fairness and good for all. The problem is that their methods are out of sync with the reality of God's perfect heart.

Their hearts will not be corrected by my social media shouting.

More likely, their hearts will be touched by the grace and love of our God, extended through friendships with those who are living according to his heart.

Adopting the biblical attitudes I have shared may cause some around you to be angry with you. Jesus gets it. His teaching and life caused great anger among those he came to save. Pray for wisdom in how to infuse grace and peace into your daily walk with others.

3. *Strive for holiness.* The pursuit of holiness in our culture is challenging. As was mentioned in the chapter on un-hacking, the nature of our electronic device, sugar, television, and other dopamine producers have produced in us a very short attention span and a tendency toward a spastic lifestyle that prevents serious devotion to our spiritual formation.

We must strive to develop our closeness to our Lord. We must reject just getting emotionally worked up through loud music and light shows along with emotion-laden preaching and instead intentionally pursue an ongoing, life-changing conversation with God in his Word and through reflective listening.

The tensions that have been aroused through our society continually banging the oppression and marginalization drum need supernatural intervention to heal. This is a hurt that will only be calmed through a supernatural, empowered Christ lover.

Identifying with Humanity—Nehemiah

There is much anger to be calmed, much guilt to assuage in the area of the mistreatment of others in our world. Much of the intensity of this has been artificially elevated by people who profit greatly from the anger and guilt.

We are left with a dangerous mess—something like an out-of-control nuclear reactor that could go completely unstable at any moment.

Following the lead of the Old Testament leader Nehemiah would be wise.

He lived in a time when his people had sinned so badly against God that most of them had been taken captive and hauled off to a foreign land. Those left back home were in bad shape. When Nehemiah heard about the horrible condition of Jerusalem and its inhabitants, he prayed a beautiful prayer to our Lord. We would do well to pray for our collective sins as his created children, just as Nehemiah did:

> I now pray before you day and night for the people of Israel your servants, confessing the sins of the people of Israel, which we have sinned against you. Even I and my father's house have sinned. We have acted very corruptly against you.[73]

We need the power of healing that only the Lord God of heaven can provide. We cannot heal the wounds present in our own strength.

May we seek the face of God, his grace, his power, and his peace.

May we adore the image of God in every bearer of it.

Dave out …

CHAPTER 6

Stop Medicalizing Normal Life

In my role as both a psychiatrist and a practicing GP, I am increasingly seeing colleagues in both disciplines labelling normal life experiences as mental illness.
—Anthony J. McElveen

My profession has gotten pretty good at terrifying (and operating on) pregnant women during what should be one of the greatest experiences in life. And we are equally proficient at dragging the elderly through all sorts of misery on the road to death.
—H. Gilbert Welch

Before you sell a drug you have to sell an illness.
—Christopher Lane

I just didn't know how fortunate I was to make it into adulthood alive.

I was never diagnosed and treated with social anxiety disorder. Close call. I could have had years of counseling, medication, and sympathy for my sufferings.

Instead I was called shy. The adults and my friends around me encouraged me to step out, learn to converse, and stop being so worried about rejection. Apparently, at the time, being a little uncomfortable in social situations was just seen as a normal trait some people possessed that could be worked through.

I recognized by watching others my age that my responses were not optimal. By the time I was in high school, my ROTC instructor had introduced me to the old classic book *How to Win Friends and Influence People,* and I was intrigued. The primary premise of the book was that if you wanted to be seen as a good conversationalist, you needed to ask questions about the average person's favorite topic—themselves. People would like you if you were interested in and listened to them. It was an intriguing idea. I found that my dad had an old copy of the book, and I read and reread the book and began trying out the techniques.

At first, it was just because I was tired of being shy, weird, and lonely. It was a technique to possibly fit in a little better and maybe have a few more friends. My motives were entirely selfish.

But in the process of applying the techniques, I discovered something about myself—I was *fascinated* by people. Soon I was talking to everyone, still a little nervous to start out the conversation, but every time I got started, I just kept asking questions. Everyone, it seemed, had a compelling story, and I just couldn't get enough.

I just didn't *know* at the time that I had a mental disorder that required a professional counselor and even some drugs. People way back in the day of my childhood operated under this strange belief that everyone faces challenges—and that was good. You grow through recognizing a weakness and then working through it to adapt and become stronger.

You might say that the hard challenges of life were seen as formative experiences through which we grow into mature, strong, and capable adults.

In fact, the more challenges you faced as a young person, the more rapidly you matured and the better and more capable you became at handling challenges.

There weren't many *disorders,* just common life experiences that you needed to change your behavior and work through. You got stronger in the process.

Silly, isn't it? Why *grow* when you can sit on the therapist's couch, pop pills, and then post the woes of your disorder on social media and get sympathy? You can live in a perpetual crisis mode and get lots of attention for your suffering. You get pegged with a disorder and are absolved of all responsibility.

Pity beats mature adulthood any day, right?

Seventy-Seven Billion Dollars?

Seventy-seven billion dollars is what we call in the South "a whole buncha money."

It was the amount discovered to have been spent for medical treatments in 2005 of normal life conditions. This includes such things as menopause, infertility, erectile dysfunction, anxiety and behavioral disorders, body image, male pattern baldness, normal sadness, obesity, sleep disorders, and substance-related disorders.[74]

Brandeis University sociologist Peter Conrad noted in a study, "We spend more on these medicalized conditions than on cancer, heart disease, or public health."[75]

Pregnancy is another medicalized condition. It is a normal life event, as is death. Sometimes the two are combined; occasionally a woman or infant dies in the process. It is tragic but has been part of the history of humankind since, well, humankind.

Dr. Gilbert Welch noted,

> Consider this. Two of the most common tests performed on pregnant American women are obstetrical ultrasound and electronic fetal monitoring. After reviewing experimental studies involving more than 27,000 women, the Cochrane review—an independent, international collaboration that summarizes evidence for medical procedures—found that late-pregnancy ultrasound "does not confer benefit on mother or baby."

But it does a good job of scaring expectant parents. Among other things, it finds minor anatomic abnormalities (like "bright spots" in the heart or intestine) that have been associated with feared genetic disorders such as Down syndrome ... The problem is that the minor anatomical abnormalities are about 30 times more common than the genetic disorders they have been associated with.

This means most parents who are told after an ultrasound that their child might have serious problems are told so needlessly. Not surprisingly, this leads to a lot of unnecessary heartache and extra testing. This has led one of the founders of the technology to write that its routine use has crossed the line and now causes "more harm than good."[76]

I had friends who experienced some of the "testing indicates that your baby has a serious genetic issue—do you want to abort" kind of scenario. In nearly every case I have been aware of, the child was normal. We do have a few family friends whose children did have some genetic issues, but those kids (some of whom are now adults) are purely wonderful human beings. So what purpose does the tests serve, given their high rate of false results?

Pregnancy should be an exciting time of bringing a new precious life into the family, but such false positives create a lot of stress for the parents—and of course stress causes the body to release cortisol, which will have an adverse effect on the developing child.

Every time my wife and I were expecting, I had this "adult" expectation of what could happen.

We could have a normal pregnancy and childbirth.

We could have a miscarriage.

My wife could die during the birthing process.

The child could be dead on delivery, during delivery, or shortly after.

The child could have a serious health issues.

Those are just some of the possible results of childbirth, and as mature adults, my wife and I accepted those potential consequences. We refused tests to detect Down's syndrome because we would not have changed anything about the pregnancy had the test been positive.

Pregnancy and its associated risks are just a normal part of life. The more normal, the better.

So why do we medicalize normal life challenges? Is it just a fear-based society? Is it that we worship at the altar of medicine and trust them too much? Is it solely tied to the profit motive of medical providers and pharmaceutical companies?

For the sake of becoming who God says we are, we need to stop medicalizing and drugging our blessings. Growth comes through suffering—and suffering is a normal experience in human life.

The ADHD Kid

I walked into my cabin at a summertime Bible camp I work at. One of the kids I was in charge of had one of the other kids down on a bunk, pummeling him with his fists.

I shouted, "Hey, stop that!"

The abusing kid stopped momentarily, looked at me incredulously, and exclaimed, "But I have ADHD!"

"Oh, I'm sorry, then just go ahead and beat the snot out of him!" I replied sarcastically.

We had a good conversation after that. This kid had learned to use his medicalized term of diagnosis in order to excuse any behavior he got in trouble for.

I suppose it worked with his family. It did not work with me.

One of my more serious concerns about medicalization regards children and teens with what is called ADHD. I've been around a

bunch of kids with the diagnosis, and I agree they have a problem—
it's just that I totally disagree with the treatment and the foundation
of the diagnosis.

I know I'll be heavily criticized by experts for this critique
of ADHD, and that is okay. Medical doctors and especially the
pseudoscience of psychology and the counseling profession are very
prone to groupthink. I've been through the training, and it has been
unfortunately compromised by being based on naturalistic evolution
(unproven dogma) and political issues (social justice). The drug
companies also make big money keeping kids on drugs for years
that I perceive, from the brain chemistry issues involved, results
in a lifetime of harm. But the reason we do this is because of the
behavior issues of the kids like the one who was beating up his friend
at Bible camp.

You can give him his ADHD drug, and he will settle down and
behave better for a while. That is, he will behave better for a few
hours. It makes it easier on us, but I fear that in the long term, it
will be devastating to him.

The ADHD Brain

I've done research on brain chemicals over the last two years,
with a heavy emphasis on the neurotransmitters dopamine and
serotonin.

Our culture provides more soothers than ever before. Some
would call them addictive items, but I prefer to call them *soothers* or
comforts. Addiction tends to give a person an excuse for their poor
discipline, rather than showing a proper internal locus of control on
something they have chosen to do and just say, "I need to get control
of this" or "I need to change the way I live." I call the numerous items
in our society that are producing too much of one brain chemical
"habituated comforts."

The brain chemical that we are getting too much of and that is
causing so much trouble is *dopamine.* Dopamine and serotonin are

both something that God designed and provided to us to make life "very good."[77]

Dopamine is pretty exciting. If you are a roller-coaster person, dopamine provides that rush you feel when you head over that first big hill. During an orgasm, a large dose of dopamine is released. Dopamine is a reward chemical, also released when we eat. Sugary foods release a lot of dopamine. Most illegal drugs and quite a few legal ones stimulate or directly provide dopamine.

Though dopamine is very good, there are some issues regarding it we need to be aware of.

It is intense, and so God designed our dopamine receptors to downregulate or "pull back / shut down" in order to protect us if we get too much of it or get the chemical too often. Because of this, overproduction of dopamine will lead to *tolerance,* a condition in which it takes increasing amounts of a stimulus in order to get the same dopamine reward.

This is part of the process of how someone becomes an alcoholic or drug addict. As the brain senses the overloads of dopamine from the excess stimulation, it downregulates the receptors, so the person who is consuming too much alcohol or taking too much of a drug ends up taking ever-increasing amounts in order to feel the same comfort/soothing effect.

If you scan their brains for dopamine-receptor activity, you will see significantly less activity in their brain than in a nonabuser's brain.

The scary part of this—if you keep up this too-much-dopamine behavior, the receptors *die!* This is bad. Dopamine and its effect are part of the joy and excitement of life God designed and gifted for us. If you are a sexually active adult, married I hope, think of not getting much enjoyment from sex with your mate. Think of an amusement park ride not doing much for you. A lot of the joy, excitement, and motivation to go forward in life is provided by dopamine.

Once you kill these receptors, life is going to be a lot harder and duller.

If you look at a kid's brain scan who has been diagnosed with ADHD, it looks very much like someone who is drug addicted, alcoholic, or obese. The dopamine receptor activity is very low.

Most if not all of the current medications for ADHD increase dopamine to the brain. Is that really a good idea?

Yes, I've seen the kids at camp. The parents even warn me that if little Bobby starts getting agitated, nervous, violent, and grabbing things, he should take his meds. It happens. I take him to the nurse, and he takes his pill, and in a few minutes, he starts calming down. The stuff works!

Well, think about this.

Heroin also releases a strong dose of dopamine. A regular heroin user will develop a tolerance pretty quickly, and their brain scan will look a lot like that of a kid with ADHD. When the addict takes more and more and runs out of money and can't get any more, he has trouble sleeping, is agitated, can get violent, and is very annoying or even dangerous to be around.

If you want to "help" him, try the following. Get a large syringe full of very high-quality heroin and let him shoot up. You will see almost an immediate improvement in his behavior. He will become calmer and less angry, and it will be a lot easier to be around him.

Now you realize, don't you, that you only helped *you* by giving him more of a dopamine rush? You have calmed him, improved his behavior for a few hours, and also contributed to the further downregulating and possible death of his dopamine receptors. You've contributed to his future misery but made him much easier to be around for a bit.

When we give a kid who has likely gotten into his ADHD condition because he is eating too much sugar, watching too much television, playing too many video games for too long, and is on a smartphone almost every waking hour—when you give him a pill that increases his dopamine, yes, he will feel the rush on his downregulated receptors, and he will calm down. He will be more easily managed. He will be less troublesome—*to you*.

And yet, have we dealt with the root cause of his agitation, violence, and lack of attention span? He has been gorging on dopamine-producing activities in life—and we are giving him a strong dopamine fix to make him *feel* and *behave* better. For a few hours?

Eventually, if we don't deal with the root causes, his receptors will die. He will miss a great portion of what constitutes motivation, reward, and joy in life.

All so that he is more pleasant to be around and so that the doctors and drug companies can buy their next Tesla and an even larger house.

The Kid Needs …

The symptoms of too much dopamine include the following:

- sleeplessness, poor quality sleep
- increased substance abuse
- increased alcoholism
- increased appetite
- poor impulse control
- increased suicidality

I mentioned serotonin earlier. What does it do and how does it *play* with dopamine?

First of all, there is a curious interaction in that too much dopamine seems to suppress serotonin. I'm simplifying all of this greatly. But if you are aggressively producing dopamine, the activities themselves tend to be at odds with the things that produce serotonin.

So, first, what does serotonin do? Here are a few things:

- increased contentment
- inhibited anger
- increased control over impulses

- lower hunger
- better quality sleep

Seems perfect for someone with ADHD symptoms that what they really need is *more serotonin, less dopamine.* How does one do that?

The kid needs, if he or she is going to recover (and not kill) their dopamine receptors, to decrease any activity that produces dopamine and choose to do those things that produce serotonin.

What produces dopamine? Here are a few common sources:

- television / streaming video
- nicotine
- pornography
- caffeine
- alcohol
- sugar
- drugs (including ADHD medications)
- shopping
- video games
- social media
- smartphones, tablets, and associated software
- gambling

The ADHD kid needs a lot less of these. In truth, each one of us needs to learn self-control, discipline, and how to be an adult. We all need to grow a spine and make the hard choices instead of playing the medicalized victim card. "I'm addicted" as an excuse needs to be replaced with "I'm making poor choices and paying the consequences."

At the same time, the ADHD kid needs to be directed and coached in choosing activities and a mindset that produce serotonin. Some of those follow:

- bright, full-spectrum light (not at night near bedtime though; think of the natural day/night cycle)
- diet
- supplements
- exercise
- self-induced mood enhancements

Why are we not leading kids who struggle with what is identified as ADHD into a lifestyle and discipline that incorporates these healthy choices?

They take time, involvement, and patience, and there isn't likely a lot of ongoing revenue to be made in this. Parents are too busy, the results take too long, and too often, the parents are dopamine junkies themselves.

We give the kid a pill. It's easy and quick. We sacrifice his future as we medicalize the consequences of a poorly chosen lifestyle that has made the kid a dopamine junkie.

This isn't just about ADHD. Other "disorders" also are related to dopamine:

- bipolar disorder (mania)
- obsessive-compulsive disorder (OCD)
- paranoia
- psychosis
- schizophrenia

The long-term impact of ADD/ADHD drugs is not well advertised. But just understanding the operation of dopamine, dopamine receptors, and serotonin should make it clear that our current medicalization of what is mostly the consequences of bad choices about habituated comforts (and in the case of children, that is a bad choice of what parents and schools let their children do with their time) is doing incredible harm.

The Nonmedicalized Solution to ADHD

This is just a perception based on the evidence. I know I do not have the research or experiential credentials that others have.

With ADHD, you have a child with all the symptoms (and the brain scan) of someone with too much dopamine exposure. You also naturally have the indications of a person who has too little serotonin.

Does it not make sense what the first possible solution that we should try is?

Realize that to try to take a kid who is agitated, perhaps violent, unfocused, and who doesn't sleep well into a dopamine-restricted, serotonin-increasing lifestyle change is going to be a real challenge. It will take at least a year to recover normal dopamine receptor activity. If he has been dopamine gorging all his life, some of his receptors may be already gone.

Bringing an immature person out of a habituated comfort situation that has produced what we call ADHD will be grueling. It is possibly going to require dedicated treatment—since the chemicals and neural pathways are pretty much identical to alcohol or drug issues.

What does this treatment look like?

Pretty much, *normal* life stops. Most adults go into a recovery program in which your activities are completely restricted—so that the addict cannot access drugs or alcohol. It is *now normal* for a young boy or girl to gorge on sugar, have their face buried in a smartphone, rarely go outside, be lonely, disconnected, and overweight, and have less of an attention span than a goldfish.

The treatment needs to establish the *machine normal* of what nourishes the biomechanical-spiritual-emotional creature was intended to flourish under.

This means good, nonsugary food, sunshine, exercise, strong family and friend relationships, reading, reflecting, and learning to direct one's thoughts and moods.

What is needed is a radical change to a healthy life. No smartphone, television, refined sugar, caffeine, sodas—the list could go on, but these things must not be available. This kid is going to be miserable for a while.

Just like any other junkie.

The parents will be miserable too.

The question is, do we want to help the child be healthy or just make the next few hours easier on the parents? Or the teachers?

Of course, the ADHD child would have to be led into a habit of serotonin-producing situations. This will be very hard as well for parents who are continually bowed in front of smartphone screens, tablets, eating and drinking their fifty pounds of refined sugar per year, and consuming alcohol once their agitated little sweetheart is in his room.

Healthy living is likely to only occur in a family and church environment.

We, as blood-bought believers, need to start trusting God and following his cues for a holistic level of health.

For those of us in the United States, the *normal* way of living is extremely antihealthy. We are the most anxious, depressed, lonely, overweight, sleep-deprived, angry, isolated, addicted, and medicated generation in the history of the world. (Heard that before in this book?)

The way out is hard.

Things worth doing are hard.

The choice lies before us.

Do what is good for the soul and the biomechanical body that is its home, or take a pill to make the next few hours easier.

To put it another way, when we see a bad result from poor choices, we can align with how God designed us to live—or we can medicalize the issue to obtain momentary relief.

ADHD Is Just One Example

If I look back on my own life, as I started this chapter with a story of, I am thankful that the routine challenges of life were not medicalized then.

In my late teen years, I began experiencing a lot of nervousness and eventually a crazy and overwhelming sense of fear. I had never heard the words *panic attack*, but I was having them. I was not aware that I had generalized anxiety disorder (GAD), but had I been born a few years later, I would have been diagnosed with that. Would that have been a good thing?

No.

As it was, I had to learn to discipline and control my thought life, my exercise regimen, my social life, and my diet, and I had to just go ahead and run into situations that caused me great fear. While it has been popular over the past couple of decades for people suffering from similar challenges to chastise people and proclaim, "Don't tell someone with anxiety to get over it," in reality, that is what you need to work to do if you have anxiety. It is called exposure therapy by those in the counseling industry.

The interesting thing about this is that a lot of our problems would be solved by living in accordance with what God designed for us as normal, going back to the comments made by Graham above.

God designed a beautiful outdoor environment full of aromas, full-spectrum light, good food, animals, and people. He created the first social group, the family, right from the get-go. Sometime later came the tabernacle, then the synagogue, and eventually the ecclesia (the church). Our Creator has always been getting us together in groups. We work best when we are regularly connected with and sharing life with people.

There is a rhythm to life. There is light and darkness. When it gets dark, some brain chemicals kick in, and we get sleepy and we rest. When the sun comes up, different chemicals cause us to waken.

Jesus demonstrated the importance of work, rest, connection, and creation. He worked hard healing and speaking but then would also get away from people to be with his Father or just to fall asleep. He had his close disciples, plus a couple (Peter and John) who were in his inmost circle of friends.

The earth has seasons. There is a time to prep the soil and plant, a time to nurture, harvest, and then a dark and cold season in which life often slows down.

In our current society, we have artificial light, heat, transportation, and other capabilities that make it easy for us to completely destroy the life-nurturing rhythms of life.

We destroy ourselves in the process.

He created two types of people, male and female. The design perfection is obvious and complementary. When we trust the one who created us and pursue marriage according to his design for the precious souls contained within these temporary biomechanical-spiritual-emotional machines we inhabit, according to the operating manual he provided (the Bible), we have our greatest potential to thrive.

Anointed to be King, Why the Delay?

If you are familiar with the story of King David in the Old Testament, consider the following. From the time that Samuel anointed David until the time he was actually made king was about fifteen years.

Why did it take so long?

Most biblical scholars believe that David was between the ages of ten and fifteen when he was anointed and around thirty when he became king.

Why did it take so long for God to make this promise come true?

In between the anointing and the crowning, a lot of tough things happened.

David fought Goliath.

He also continued keeping his father's sheep.

He played harp for King Saul.

He fought and won major battles for King Saul.

King Saul got jealous and repeatedly tried to kill David, chasing him all over Israel.

David lived with a bunch of malcontents and led them into becoming "mighty men."

Why wouldn't God just anoint him and make him king of Israel on the same day?

Because David wasn't prepared yet.

God permitted a lot of tough situations to confront David to better prepare him for the mission he needed him to perform. He loved David too much to throw him into a role for which he was not prepared.

David, as a shepherd, loved God and had great enthusiasm—but he would need to learn to roam the wilderness and live off the land. He would need to learn to trust God when everything seemed dark and impossible.

One of the great things about David is that he was a prolific writer, and his struggles and victories are poetically recorded in the Psalms. Consider the following powerful poem that teaches us the value of wisdom that can only be learned through suffering:

> Truly God is good to Israel, to those who are pure in heart.
> But as for me, my feet had almost stumbled.
> For I was envious of the arrogant when I saw the prosperity of the wicked.
> For they have not pangs until death; their bodies are fat and sleek.
> They are not in trouble as others are; they are not stricken like the rest of mankind.
> Therefore pride is their necklace; violence covers them as a garment.

> Their eyes swell out through fatness; their hearts
> overflow with follies.
> They scoff and speak with malice; loftily they
> threaten oppression.[78]

David is just raw with his perception of injustice. The world just seems totally unfair, and he is questioning why he is even trying.

It is as if David is sitting down over coffee with us, sharing this enormous struggle of making sense of how, in his devotion to God, things could be so hard.

His answer comes shortly:

> But when I thought how to understand this, it
> seemed to me a wearisome task, until I went into
> the sanctuary of God; then I discerned their end.
> Truly you set them in slippery places; you make
> them fall to ruin.
> How they are destroyed in a moment, swept away
> utterly by terrors!
> Like a dream when one awakes, O Lord, when you
> rouse yourself, you despise them as phantoms.
> When my soul was embittered, when I was pricked
> in heart, I was brutish and ignorant; I was like a
> beast toward you.[79]

Like a beast?

Sometimes today, being a *beast* means you really conquered something, but it is an interesting choice of word for David in his time.

Understanding the challenge of living as a spiritual being temporarily encased in a physical body requires us to grasp what the apostle Paul called the challenge of the *flesh*. The flesh is best understood as that portion of us that is most animal-like.

If a male dog is out walking and smells a female dog in heat, he just goes and mates with her—and continues on his business. He doesn't reflect on the quality of the relationship or any of God's commands about sexuality and the holiness of our spirits. That's not really in a dog's wheelhouse. He's just a beast.

When we face challenges and medicalize them, are we not being beastly? We feel anxious, so we drink a glass of wine. Or we take antianxiety meds. We do not consider and reflect on the underlying issues causing our anxiety. We do not seek God and his wisdom to grow into a holistic peace—something known as *shalom* to Jewish people.

We just seek comfort from pain.

The male dog mounts the female.

Beastly and unwise behavior.

We, as blood-bought believers, must stop being beasts and satisfying the flesh. We must stop medicalizing our blessings.

Dave out …

CHAPTER 7

Traditions versus Traditionalism

Though historically the Christian church has taught that the spiritual life ascends
through stages, many believers today have never heard of this truth. In fact,
it sounds elitists or even prideful to man—with the result that contemporary,
Westernized Christianity focuses far more on conversion than on transformation.
—Gary Thomas

The Church has real issues, but Jesus still refers to the Church as His body,
His Bride! We must love His Bride, not gripe about her or leave her.
—Francis Chan

The gravest question before the Church is always God Himself, and the
most portentous fact about any man is not what he at a given time may
say or do, but what he in his deep heart conceives God to be like.
—A.W. Tozer

On this rock I will build my church, and the gates
of hell shall not prevail against it.
—Jesus of Nazareth[80]

~~~~~~

The music was loud, and the light show spectacular. The drum beat was pounding my ears and chest. The crowd was on its feet (mostly), and most had at least one hand if not two raised to the sky in praise.

My wife and I were at a large Christian conference in Atlanta.

There was a praise/music team on stage before each speaker. It had the vibe of a massive rock concert.

Standing and raising hands in praise to God is a good thing—although not really part of my worship tradition. So my wife and I were sitting, praising God from our seats—well, sort of. I was also observing the twenty-something-year-old fellow believers in front of me.

They were standing with one or two arms raised—in praise?

I could hear their conversation even over the loud music.

"We could go to the taco truck."

"I saw Italian out there. We haven't tried that yet."

"Would you rather drive off campus and go to a real restaurant?"

In my church family, there are some sweet people who want to go more *contemporary* and do the loud music, light show, fog machine, and stand with arms raised style of "worship." They feel it is more *authentic* and would generate more passion for Jesus.

But what was happening at this event—with my food-obsessed brothers and sisters *standing with arms raised,* as well as with me and my wife *sitting and worshipping with our arms in a relaxed position,* should give us pause.

Believers often choose churches based upon the worship style—thinking that one is better than the other, more authentic, or even more biblical.

And perhaps you have a strong opinion on this as well?

Perhaps you think my wife and I are just *not getting it* by our outwardly dull approach to church. Maybe you favor the stand and raise hands approach with the rock band and light show.

Or perhaps you believe, as some in my church family, that we should *not* be standing and raising our hands, or even have the loud bands and trendy/authentic-looking people on stage putting on a rock-style concert.

In either case, on most Sundays in the West, and on some Saturday evenings, there is great noise and spectacle generated in the name of church. A whole bunch of people pack into buildings and homes at certain times of the week and do *worship*.

Can I be your Dave? Can I dare suggest that we are emphasizing entirely the wrong elements of church? Can we go to scripture together and see that what we value in this ecclesia process is mostly wrongheaded?

Throughout the history of the Christian faith, there have been many attempts to put the church on the *right* footing, from the reformation to restoration, home church movement, and perhaps even to the community church movement. They have all had some good results—and some not so good consequences as well.

There is a lesson there, of course. As one preacher I heard a few years ago said, "Where there's people, there's problems!" Much of the New Testament letters are at least in part dealing with serious problems going on in the faith community the letter is addressed to.

Or, as with the letters to Timothy, letters to a young preacher as he deals with discouraging issues with his faith community.

Realize that *problem people* (as we shall see more fully in this chapter) are part of the reason the church exists. As many have said before in the faith, God loves you where you are, but he doesn't want you to stay where you are. What he seeks, and what I pray we desire, is *transformation*.

Let's just get it out front—the perfect church is imperfect, because part of the mission of the church is to transform ordinary pagans into sanctified and joyous warriors for righteousness.

But then there is the *big tradition*. For so many of us, even in a home church environment, the big tradition has been impacting our expectations and form of worship—simply because we do not even think to question it.

Even in a home church, we come together and sit facing a leader of some sort—the preacher, song leader, or pastor. We are the audience, and there is a traditional and particular structure of worship.

As mentioned earlier, perhaps you are expected to stand with your arms held high during the music. Or maybe you are *not* supposed to do that in order to show proper reverence. Maybe the one who shares the message shouts and enunciates his words in a very dramatic fashion, and the listeners shout back, "Amen!" and "Preach!" responses. Or maybe the sermon is delivered in a very calm but serious demeanor.

There are expectations in nearly all faith communities of a structured worship service and the elements of that. And that is not necessarily wrong, but the bigger question is, are we accomplishing the mission of our local church in the process of observing this big tradition of structured ecclesias?

The big tradition, which still influences us without much recognition, goes back to the events of the third century—when something that seemed very good, even victorious, happened that took the church in a direction that it had never really been in before.

An intense persecution broke out against believers, as recorded in the book of Acts. It worsened after the burning of Rome as Nero and his administration attempted to place the blame on believers in the Christ and the killing of disciples became officially sanctioned.

The ecclesia began to thrive.

It would seem that the truism "that which we obtain lightly we esteem little" was true for those early believers. Following the Christ could cost you everything—but it was worth it.

While we are discussing that truth, just take a minute to honestly evaluate whether or not the faith you conceive in your heart is something worth suffering and dying for. If not, why not? What is missing in your understanding of our mutual faith that would keep you from standing for Yeshua of Nazareth, the King of the universe, right now? Perhaps it is our view of our Lord himself that is inadequate.

Back to our first- and second-century brothers and sisters. There was something about being *in Christ* and in his church that was worth it all, and the church grew in strength and power.

But in the third century, something happened that would lead to the church adopting the methodologies and traditions of pagan religions. Its impact continues to this day—in my own church family and probably yours.

A Roman emperor converted to Christianity and made following Christ the official religion of the state. Emperor Constantine became a believer.

I can imagine that those believers in his day were celebrating. Their persecuted status was likely coming to an end. God had achieved a major victory!

But I think Satan was celebrating even more—for Constantine, as an emperor, was seen by many (perhaps even himself?) to be a god or nearly so, and he decided to *give* some things to his Christian brothers and sisters, probably because his pagan religious traditions made him feel that church would be better, more religious, if it had these elements.

Buildings, Vestments, Idols, and Mystic Priests

Constantine, in making Christianity the official religion, gave many of the pagan temples to his fellow believers. The once-persecuted, underground, and tight-knit group of strugglers for the kingdom of God suddenly had a nice temple, and they could walk to it in broad daylight and enter in dignity.

Along with it came the religious vestments, special garments that separated some believers from others. A special class of experts, those who first donned the garments, were now looked to as having special knowledge and authority within the called out of God.

Thus was born the church "audience," who were subjected to the "service" presented to the "lay" people. Clergy, those in "the ministry," became a thing. And laity, the people to whom the service, sacraments, and words were delivered, became the audience.

For too many of our churches to this day, this model has been hard to escape.

It is preventing us, as the warrior bride of Christ, from

understanding that *we* (each of us) are members of the royal priesthood[81] and that *each of us* has a holy mission to embrace the covenant of reconciliation,[82] to tear down strongholds, and to destroy arguments[83] raised against the knowledge of our holy God.

We are, each of us and together, to be the body of Christ on earth. If all we do is show up and worship by standing with hands raised or by sitting reverently, we are not being the body. We are to be actively engaged in the mission of our Lord's church every day in every way. The gates of hell must be assaulted!

Further, there are many admonishments made (around fifty) about the nature of how we do church in terms of our responsibilities to love and nourish *one another* to increasingly higher levels of maturity.

Here's a big question in light of the outward mission as well as the inward transformational purpose of the bride of Christ—how's that working out in our big tradition-laden churches?

Are *you* and your everyday *our* (that we are supposed to be—remember the "our," not "my," principle) actually daily engaging the reconciliation of the lost all around you? Are we destroying the strongholds raised against our Lord's kingdom by loving the Lord with all our hearts, souls, and minds?[84]

If not, what are we doing? Just going to be the audience, getting emotionally worked up by a moving and clever sermon from a trendily dressed pastor, feeling better about ourselves, and then going on with our walk in life as a slightly more polite pagan while speaking some Jesus words?

Is our church service nothing more than a performance that glorifies a speaker, a praise team, and makes us feel emotionally better about ourselves? If so, are we really worshipping, or are we just serving a system? Are we just worshipping ourselves? Is the reason the church has so little impact in our world, given its size, just that we have not been the ecclesia and instead have become an audience enjoying the work of talented performers?

Dean Inserra, in his thought-provoking book *Getting Over*

Yourself: Trading Believe-In-Yourself Religion for Christ-Centered Christianity, notes,

> Don't get me wrong; I love church music. I love the music at the church where I pastor. I also prefer good stage lighting and rock bands as my style choice for a Sunday morning. But I absolutely believe that singing the Word together as a congregation is the point. It is not a concert. Something different has happened in pop-Christianity that has turned music into more than congregational singing. It is now an experience with higher expectations than the quality and content of the sermon ... Author Mike Cosper writes, "Celebrity culture turns pastors and worship leaders into icons. Celebrity culture turns worship gatherings into rock concerts. Celebrity culture confuses flash and hype for substance." These services, Cosper adds, are an "emotional ride lead by a hip, handsome, and passionate rock star." The music is followed by a "communicator" whose message, as Aaron Armstrong wrote, "seems to be less about what Jesus has done for you and is doing in you, and more about what you are doing to unlock, release, and call down God's blessing and realize your life potential."[85]

They may wear traditional vestments, or perhaps skinny jeans and too-tight untucked shirts, but the emphasis is on a performance to make you *feel* holy and bring glory to *your* life. We have a large number of superstar pastors and worship leaders now. Too bad Jesus isn't the superstar, eh?

The David Principle and the Church

Young David was out watching the sheep. He was the youngest brother, not very well thought of, and doing the job that was given to the least valuable person in the family. Sheep are frustrating, fearful, and obstinate little creatures. The days (and nights) are long for a shepherd. But David was faithful, even defending these stupid little creatures from the attacks of wild animals.[86]

One day, one of his older brothers ran out and brought him to a special meeting with the prophet Samuel. He is brought in front of this special man of the age, who proceeds to anoint him with oil; he is to be the king of Israel.

And so he was, right? No, not exactly. As we mentioned earlier, David was not yet prepared to be a king.

What would follow was a weird journey of victories and defeats, suffering and hiding, and eventually, he *would* be the king.

But at one point while he was serving as a valiant warrior for King Saul following the defeat of Goliath—the people are singing praises for a military victory and give a greater number of credits for dead people to David than they do to Saul—Saul became enraged. Eventually, David had to run away and spend a lot of time hiding.

During this time when David is on the run from Saul, the following is recorded:

> David departed from there and escaped to the cave of Adullam. And when his brothers and all his father's house heard it, they went down there to him. And everyone who was in distress, and everyone who was in debt, and everyone who was bitter in soul, gathered to him. And he became commander over them. And there were with him about four hundred men.[87]

Did you ever have that experience in school on the playground, when you were being forced to play kickball or some other sport, and two kids got to pick the teams, one kid at a time? Of course, they pick their friends, the best athletes, and maybe the prettiest girls first. (Yep, I was none of those, so I was *always* the last guy chosen.)

David gets brought a team to be commander of. They are distressed, in debt, and bitter people.

Awesome, right?

This group of rabble became the core of what would be known as the "mighty men," an incredible and nearly unstoppable group of warriors that David led into battle.

But the *mighty* started as a *mighty flawed and annoying group of whiners.* These people were seriously messed up.

There is a theological principle called *typology* in which our Creator provides us with a visual and literal representation of a spiritual truth. I perceive that this may be one of them, and it involves what the church is supposed to be. David and his band of malcontents are transformed into mighty men. A bunch of bitter and weak men become an unstoppable force for the purposes of God.

That's a "type" of what the ecclesia of our Lord is to be! We are the rabble, the weak, the indebted, the bitter and unhappy people called into a cave to follow—a dynamic superstar pastor?

No, to follow the indwelling Holy Spirit, the magnificent, inspired Word of God, and the encouragement provided by being a part of one another—to become an unstoppable projection of God's power in a lost and dying world.

Because of the big tradition, our efforts in this area are largely handicapped. For the most part, there is clergy and laity. Even in my church tradition, where we deny there is such a thing as clergy or laity, the distinction exists. The laity tends to go to be the audience and then lie around like pagans (slightly more polite but just as untransformed) the rest of the time. The clergy is on stage, increasingly dressed in a manner that conforms with the superstar persona in the world, and they perform for the audience. We praise their speaking, singing, or playing ability, and we the audience feel a bit holier. But we are not transformed, just hyped up. We the laity return to the big show a week later, feel a little better about ourselves, and go on about our daily life as polite and slightly improved pagans.

The church consumers speak much of what "my pastor said" and perhaps comment on how great the music was, but rarely do we hear believers today say, "I was studying the book of Ezekiel, and I found this precept of God that really penetrated my heart."

I mean, who in churches today reads Ezekiel? Who thinks?

Most preachers/pastors/priests I have known personally would be thrilled to hear their fellow believers speaking of their own time in the Word in a deep way.

It just doesn't happen much.

Sundays are characterized by lots of noise and spectacle in western churches. But in spite of the number of churches and believers, there is very little significant impact.

Mission *not* accomplished.

Paralyzed from the Mouth Down

Dave here again. Brace yourself.

Paul, in the first letter to the church at Corinth, shares the following vitally important truth:

> For in one Spirit we were all baptized into one body—Jews or Greeks, slaves or free—and all were made to drink of one Spirit.

> For the body does not consist of one member but of many. If the foot should say, "Because I am not a hand, I do not belong to the body," that would not make it any less a part of the body. And if the ear should say, "Because I am not an eye, I do not belong to the body," that would not make it any less

a part of the body. If the whole body were an eye, where would be the sense of hearing? If the whole body were an ear, where would be the sense of smell? But as it is, God arranged the members in the body, each one of them, as he chose. If all were a single member, where would the body be? As it is, there are many parts, yet one body.[88]

Just being honest, I think in my church life we have had too much mouth, too much ear, and too little hands and feet. Way too little brain. We talk some good talk; after all, it is based on the eternal and enduring truth of scripture.

We sit and listen to preaching as an ear. It makes us feel something, and we say, "What a talented preacher!" We listen to music performed from a stage and get emotionally fired up, and we say, "What a great band! Praise God!" It stirs us emotionally for a few minutes and meets a felt need.

Or in my faith tradition, we all sing because we are commanded to, and then we say we did what was required of us. This is a principle I disagree with biblically, by the way.

But in this superstar-audience-service model of worship, we do not accomplish what David and his band of unhappy slobs did. They all (David and his rabble band) were transformed into an elite group of warriors pursuing the purposes of God in bringing the Messiah into the world.

Once their transformation achieved some traction, they left their cave and fought the battles that needed to be fought.

They obviously encouraged one another to grow in courage in the pursuit of what God wanted done.

The leadership of David was vital, but it only worked when he actually stayed knit together with God—as some of his less than stellar moments prove.

God elevated David at his pleasure. David was at his best when he glorified God and stayed close to his side.

One of my favorite sayings of David reflects his heart when it was right before God, not glorifying or platforming himself, and it brings me to tears when I say it honestly before our God as well:

> Who am I, O Lord God, and what is my house, that you have brought me thus far? And yet this was a small thing in your eyes, O Lord God. You have spoken also of your servant's house for a great while to come, and this is instruction for mankind, O Lord God! And what more can David say to you? For you know your servant O Lord God! Because of your promise, and according to your own heart, you have brought about all this greatness, to make your servant know it. Therefore you are great, O Lord God. For there is none like you, and there is no God besides you, according to all that we have heard with our ears.[89]

In this moment, David is overwhelmed with the faithful hand of God in his life. He knows where his entire life, provision, strength, and all good things have come from. And he is overwhelmed with gratitude and amazement.

It is the story of *my* life.

I've done a fair amount of preaching over the years (not my primary line of work, by the way), but I *have* been teaching Bible class for more than three decades. Recently while teaching, I could tell the message was really resonating with the precious people I was speaking to, and the Spirit prompted me to say, "If you come away from this class thinking, *Steve is a great teacher,* I have absolutely failed. The message is that you should be convicted that we serve a great and powerful, ever-present God, and my goal is that you be excited to get up in the morning to pursue the kingdom mission with him."

There is something about drawing a large group of people who want to hear me speak, who compliment me generously on a "great class," and yes it does appeal to a part of me that is still that kid who was always the last chosen on the playground.

Yes, part of me desires to be seen as intelligent, spiritual, dynamic, and powerful and to be the speaker of choice—but those words of David always bring me back to reality.

I'm the weak one.

I'm the *weakest one.*

I was born a shy, not so bright, uncoordinated, lanky, awkward, comfort-seeking, scared little boy. I failed miserably at almost everything I tried, and when I had nearly destroyed myself, I put my hands up to God and repeated (unknowingly) the most beautiful prayer in the Bible: "Lord, help me!"[90]

This statement is from the Canaanite woman who had a demon-possessed daughter. She came to Jesus and tried to flatter him into helping her, probably a tactic she had used with other men in her life. She called him "O Lord, Son of David," so she apparently had done at least a little research on him; she knew he had power, knew he was a "son of David," and tried to win her way into some help for the daughter she loved.

Jesus ignored her.

It was then that she fell at his feet and said, "Lord, help me."

Even then, he had to make sure she saw who she was without him. He mentioned to her that he wasn't sent to the "dogs," a common moniker applied to non-Jews by Jews.

She had a brutal and honest look into her heart and said, "Yes, Lord."

She was a "dog." Not in the sense of a cute and pampered pet like we have now. In her society, dogs were mangy, disease-riddled pests that were a threat to your life.

She agreed that was her. "Lord, help me."

Lord, help us all. We all start out as stinky, flesh-obsessed, comfort-seeking dogs.

Our churches, I perceive, need to stop platforming talented

people and putting on a show. We need the help of the Lord to help us avoid the sin of self-idolatry due to the talents and abilities he has given some of us.

I seem to have been given a measure of ability in writing and speaking that resonates with people. I'm thankful.

I'm grateful.

But I do need to remember that without Yeshua as my Savior, I was a mangy, disease-ridden mutt on a path to self-destruction. He has chosen to show grace to me by working through me—but the power is his and his alone.

Big Church Issues

Please do not get me wrong—I'm not suggesting that you need to quit your church because it is big. That has been tried and found lacking. Small churches and even *home* churches fall prey to the old "big church" pagan issues of clergy/laity distinctions, superstar members, and the wrong audience (once again, the Trinity is our only audience), just as often as big church systems do.

But we need to think through some of the following issues in light of what scripture reveals to us about being the body of Christ:

1. Numbers. Back to our friend King David. There is a story that is so powerful, yet I rarely hear it discussed in my particular church family. It has always been a tradition that during services and Bible class time, there are men who walk around counting noses; the attendance is taken, recorded, and, in many congregations, posted on a wall (or website) for all to see.

What is it we are trying to do? Do we believe our strength, spiritual health, or worth as the body of Christ is determined by our numbers?

The incident with David is very curious, and the Bible, in its typical fashion, presents the facts very briefly, leaving us to prayerfully contemplate what was wrong in Israel's and David's hearts when this sin occurred.

The story begins in 2 Samuel, chapter 24, noting that "the anger of the LORD was kindled against Israel, and he incited David against them, saying, 'Go, number Israel and Judah.' So the king said to Joab, the commander of the army, who was with him, 'Go through all the tribes of Israel, from Dan to Beersheba, and number the people, that I may know the number of the people.'"[91]

In reading about Joab, I do not sense that he was necessarily a spiritual giant, but he instantly recognized that something about this idea was just dead wrong:

> May the LORD your God add to the people a
> hundred times as many as they are, while the eyes
> of my lord the king still see it, but why does my lord
> the king delight in this thing?[92]

Joab knows from what he has seen with David and the army that their victories did not occur because of superior numbers. Their victories came through the power, grace, and wisdom of God Almighty. Even Joab instantly recognized that to seek to know the strength of Israel through the numbering of the fighting men was a spurious metric. He pleaded with David not to even think in this way.

I long ago took a lesson from this story, and from all of the stories in the Bible, that God can accomplish more through twenty believers on fire for God than through two thousand pew sitters.

Audiences are consumers. Unless God is the audience.

Mighty men and women of God who love the Lord with all their hearts, souls, and minds are motivated to assault the gates of hell to accomplish the loving will of their Lord. Mighty men and women are an army fighting for the beautiful audience of one.

So why are we counting noses?

Can we just stop?

Our strength is not in numbers; our strength is found in the power that flows through and around us as indwelt children of God, working as the body of Christ.

Enough said?

2. *Understanding high worship.*

Stand with raised hands or sit reverently? Which is it?

I appeal to you to read these words of Paul and be changed in your concept of *worship:*

> I appeal to you therefor, brothers, by the mercies of God, to present your bodies as a living sacrifice, holy and acceptable to God, which is your spiritual worship.[93]

There are several terms used throughout the Bible to describe *worship*—but may I propose that this is the highest form?

This concept of being a *living sacrifice*—think about the symbology.

When a young lamb, perfect and without blemish, was offered under the terms of the Old Testament covenant, how much of it was given? Was the person offering the animal able to specify "just a leg" for God?

No, the sacrifice was total. The whole, beautiful little lamb was given.

While some of the other terms for worship, both in the Hebrew and Greek language, involve reverence, bowing, and other acts of what we consider worship, think of the significance of what the apostle Paul is describing.

Total sacrifice is not being a consumer at a rock concert–style emotion-driven superstar-pastor and worship leader performance. After all, that whole commotion is designed to appeal to the consumer.

Total sacrifice is living every moment of every day as a dead person brought to life by the indwelling Creator of all, continually seeking to join God in whatever he is doing, wherever he is doing it, out of our adoration of who he is and what he has done for us.

High worship occurs when a man chooses to do what is received as love for his wife, even when he feels neglected or misunderstood. He chooses to do what needs to be done not from an emotional high but from the heart and head knowledge that Yeshua the Christ saved him in every way that a man can be saved, and from the overwhelming sense that that sort of love is undeserved and incomprehensible, yet it is real. His inseverable love and admiration of God drives his love toward his wife, not some fleeting chemical response or a desire for reciprocal love.

High worship occurs when a young, busy mother reaches out to a difficult neighbor because she sees the pain and isolation of a life without God—and she realizes that the only thing different between herself and this dejected neighbor is the love and grace of God, "which he *lavished upon us*."[94] She recognizes that her Savior did not make a mistake in placing her in a home next to this dejected and hurting person, so she is compelled by love to reach out in spite of her too busy life. She is worshipping; her body, her very life, is her sacrifice.

The apostles Peter and John demonstrate this high worship in something I have come to call the "stewardship of what God puts in front of me" over the years. In Acts, chapter 3, the two are heading to the temple "at the hour of prayer."[95]

Think about it. Is this not somewhat similar to our going to church? They are on their way to worship, right?

Along the way is an obstruction, a delay, a roadblock to proceeding to worship. There is a man who has been unable to walk since he was born, and he calls out to Peter and John, asking for some money.

What should they do? Shouldn't they push on past this poor guy and get to worship, since it is so important?

Well, they did go on to the temple, but in this idea of *stewardship of what God puts in front of you,* perhaps their Lord had them on the way to the time of prayer in order to put them on the path to this crippled man. They didn't give the man what he asked for (money), but they gave him what he needed—the presence of the power of God.

They engaged in *high worship.*

Our time together as a church family is a form of worship, and it is vital. Remember, he is "our Father," not "my Father." The church is the bride and the very body of Christ. Whether our church is large or small, we must, as the rabble Jesus has called out, get together (as seen for the reason below) for extended periods of time.

But we must see every day of our life as an act of worship. We must see every interaction or event as potentially spiritual and kingdom related. To the point, we must know God's Word well enough to discern if a spiritual event is holy (from the Lord) or demonic (from Satan and his demons); remember, the adversary or our Lord is always prowling about.

Ask our Father to open your eyes to the *high worship* opportunities he is placing in your path as you walk with him in your everyday life.

3. *Rethinking building-centered church.*

Don't misread me on this. I'm not just advocating for the home church movement. I've seen multiple home church failures and collapses over the years—because the answer isn't polarized.

The question isn't big, small, or home.

The question is, *what form of gathering meets the covenant mission of the church where we are in the most powerful manner?*

The essential aspect of the form of meeting place for a local ecclesia is to ensure that we are fulfilling the "to one another" admonishments found throughout scripture in order to transform the rabble into the fighting force that zealously assaults the gates of hell.

The *to one another* imperatives, over fifty distinct ones, are key to how we transform from rabble to courageous warriors for the covenant mission of our Lord and Savior. I'm not going to allow you to be a baby bird and list all of them. Get in the Word yourself and write them down, meditate on them, and start doing them.

But for example, one of the biggies in our disconnected and lonely society today is found in Galatians 6:2: "Bear one another's burden, and so fulfill the law of Christ."

In our anxious, depressed, addicted, lonely, sleep-deprived, and suicidal generation, is it not the burdens weighing down disconnected people in the church that are keeping God's people from becoming the mighty men and women that God intends us to be?

Whether in a megachurch or home church, or something in between, does your church's gathering times allow for your precious people to come to know and trust one another enough, and have enough time, to share the biggest burdens (and small ones too) of life? These burdens—the sins, the fears, the loneliness—these are the spiritual obstructions that keep us seeking comfort through social media, bad food, porn, gambling, alcohol, tattoos, affairs, and other pleasure-inducing thieves that keep us wrapped up in ourselves and away from being transformed into living vessels containing the indwelling Holy Spirit of God.

The question is not big or small, home or building, or even about the worship style.

The question is, are we able to know, trust, and be with one another to fully engage the *to one another* directives? God's army is like any other army; the training and preparation for our mission is always ongoing. We should always be bringing new potential warriors into the fold and engaging them in transformational discipleship.

If you have more than about fifty members, you are going to have to have some serious small-group structure. There must be a way for the sinful rabble to spend intimate time getting to know and becoming known—and to transform one another through our continual fellowship and encouragement.

If your church structure, whatever it looks like, does not do this, work to change it. Study, meditate, and plan to fulfill the *to one another* passages.

One more item on the building-centered church.

One question we need to ask is vital. Some good friends of mine from a nearby church family established a mission in Central America. They went down numerous times to work with and to evangelize new believers in the area. They built a church building for them. They went down later and put in an electrical system for lights and fans. They went back again to make repairs.

Noble effort—but what they actually did was export *American church* to a place that likely will never be able to sustain that *system* without outside help.

Shouldn't we instead seek to establish churches who can sustain themselves? Could a small group of believers procure real estate for a decent-sized building in Chicago today? Real estate and construction prices are through the roof. Is it necessary to have a building?

Scripturally and historically, as was mentioned earlier, the church didn't really own property until the tragic day that Constantine gave it to them. Then started the big church, clergy and laity, audience and performer tradition.

We have largely been shackled to the *system* ever since.

Big churches can pool their resources and do a lot of good, but then again, so can small home churches who are in loving, unified fellowship on mission for Christ.

Whatever your church form, build a structure that empowers the believers to *love one another through the one another principles.*

Dave out ...

CHAPTER 8

If You're Not Failing, You're Not Trying

Failure should be our teacher, not our undertaker. Failure is delay, not defeat. It is a temporary detour, not a dead end. Failure is something we can avoid only by saying nothing, doing nothing, and being nothing.
—Dennis Waitley

Only those who dare to fail greatly can ever achieve greatly.
—Robert F. Kennedy

Failure isn't fatal, but failure to change may be.
—John Wooden

The Lord said to Joshua, "Get up! Why have you fallen on your face?
—God Almighty, Creator of All

had this idea, a really great idea.

It was a kingdom idea, and I was thrilled about it.

I was running the marriage-enrichment program at my church and had a number of very well-received marriage seminars and classes. I knew the divorce and suffering rate was pretty high and that my idea would be huge to our community. This would be a great opportunity to share the wisdom of God about beautiful and lasting relationships with the unchurched.

126

God was going to be impressed.

I rented a local facility. It was a beautiful place, centrally located in our town, and easy to get to. I bought a great sound and video projection system. I had a good friend of mine who is a videographer come and record the event. I did a local radio show about the event. We placed ads in the local paper and on social media and even handed out tickets.

I looked people in the eye, including one lesbian couple, who excitedly told me they would be there and couldn't wait.

On the appointed day, we set up and waited.

And waited.

We ended up with a total attendance of—wait for it—zero.

Failure much?

No. Many of my friends expressed their sympathy for the failure, but I told them what I had come to know through God's Word; striving to do great things for God is a success unto itself. Allow me to illustrate through an amazing story in the Bible.

Joshua Asks, "Why?"

Joshua was Moses's successor to lead Israel. He was a real man's man. Courageous, faithful, and up to a point, he seemed unstoppable.

Up to the city of Ai. The story is found in Joshua 7.

Ai was not a big deal. When Joshua sent out spies to check out this little town, they came back with some great news:

> Do not have all the people go up and attack Ai.
> Do make the whole people toil up there, for they
> are few.[96]

This was not really going to be a battle. Most everyone could stay in camp while just a few warriors went up and easily took the city.

Except it didn't go well:

> So about three thousand men went up there from
> the people. And they fled before the men of Ai, and
> the men of Ai killed about thirty-six of their men
> and chased them before the gate as far as Shebarim
> and struck them at the descent. And the hearts of
> the people melted and became as water.[97]

Joshua and his army failed because there had been a major sin committed by one of the men. There was a purpose in the failure—to show Israel that not trusting God for everything (one of the men had taken some valuables for himself during a previous action, not trusting God to give him what he needed) was in fact an affront to the loving nature of God.

We children of God often get hardheaded and fearful, and we justify whatever it is we think we need to do.

For that matter, we often give God's blessing to *our plans*; of course the "god" we are referring to is our own little self.

Everyone needs a good, swift kick in the rear every now and then to remind us of who we are not.

The point here is that failure is often necessary to prepare us for what God really wants to happen. Immediately after the hearts of the people became like water and Joshua was grieving and asking God, why,[98] he got a rebuke from the Lord of all:

> Get up! Why have you fallen on your face? Israel
> has sinned; they have transgressed my covenant that
> I commanded them; they have taken some of the
> devoted things.[99]

In this case, the failure was due to a serious spiritual issue that had to be dealt with. It may seem harsh, but if we could see the

Dread Sovereign Lord even in part of his glory for just a moment, he would overwhelm us.

The common reaction to anyone encountering God in any form was to fall on the ground and hide their faces in the dust.

In my case, given my own natural arrogance and stupidity in the past, I can think of God taking my life, and my only response is "Why has he been so patient with me to begin with?"

"For all have sinned and fallen short of the glory of God"[100] is the simple reality each of us must deal with. God isn't here to glorify us, although he often does in his great mercy. But we can only be glorified when we allow ourselves to be subsumed in him.

Sin must be rooted out of our hearts, and that process is painful. Sin is failure, and sometimes we fail because we are on a sinful path.

In the case of my great idea and the expensive community marriage event I put on, I perceive God was letting me try something to allow me to understand a truth I needed to learn. What was really needed from his church in my community was not a superstar speaker at some well-run event for a lot of people.

What is really needed is for the church to be the body and for each person to reach out to their neighbors in their homes, over the backyard grill, or at the kitchen table. We need to develop strong relationships with the people we live and work among and speak the good news of the Christ to them. While speaking the words to a large audience seems desirable, real impact in an isolated and lonely world will be accomplished in the same manner that Jesus showed us—he sat and ate with sinners.

I'm thankful for my big kingdom failure. It took my mind off of a big idea that *I* thought would be great for God's kingdom and onto other efforts.

So the Message Is …

If fear of failing keeps you from attempting big, hairy, audacious goals for God, then the message from our Lord is this: "Get up! Why have you fallen on your face?"[101]

People may make fun of you or exclude you when you make a big oopsie for the kingdom.

So what?

Who were you doing it for anyway?

Are you *trying* to get people to think well of you?

If so, hear the words of the Christ in his great sermon:

> Beware of practicing your righteousness before other people in order to be seen by them, for then you will have no reward from your Father who is in heaven.[102]

I perceive that the majority of people in the world and in the church are desperately insecure. I do so because *I was for so long.* Because of insecurities, other people are afraid of embarrassment through their failures and try not to fail, and often fail to even try, to preserve their image that they hope you hold of them. As one of my best friends says, "We try to hide our brokenness from broken people."[103]

Can we just realize that even if we succeed in doing something great for the kingdom of God, some will be critical of us—for the very reason that our success seems to diminish who they are? The approval of man is a very tricky and fickle thing. You get made fun of if you fail, and hated if you succeed.

Can we just trust in God's love for our approval and worth, whether we fail or succeed?

Isn't that the beautiful thing about God and our efforts?

The beautiful thing about my big idea and its absolute failure is that I perceive that God knew this idea was strong in my heart. He wanted me to step forward and try it because he wanted me to clear my heart of something that, while noble, was not in accordance with what Jesus showed us in his life.

What a God!

Was I embarrassed? No. I realized that it could be a total flop from the get-go.

I realized it because I have been a professional "fail-er" all my life. I estimate that around 80 percent of what I have tried to do exploded dramatically.

It brings tears to my eyes, but they are tears of overwhelming joy.

That God can and chooses to use the last guy chosen for everything, the guy who fails at just about everything, just because of who *he* is and in his great mercy—I love this God!

Dream big, y'all. Dream big, hairy, audacious goals for God. Try greatly, fail greatly, and then get up and try some more! Fail some more. Sit before God each morning in your armor-up time and let him help you strap on your breastplate and helmet over your bruised and bleeding body. He's not going to push you out the door. Instead, he will say, "Stick close to me, beloved!" as he leads you out onto the battlefield again.

Dave Here …

Can I be your Dave?

We in the church have lived in fear for way too long. Scripture is abundantly clear. I do not believe I can be a better Dave than the apostle John when he said,

> There is no fear in love, but perfect love casts out fear. For fear has to do with punishment, and whoever fears has not been perfected in love. We love because he has first loved us.[104]

Kick fear to the curb. Trust that God's love for you is firm and that approval of man is not worth the effort or even attainable. Humans are fickle and sinful.

God is loving, beautiful, and awesome.

Get out there and fail greatly for God.

The victories will be sweet!

Dave out …

CHAPTER 9

Ditch the Cape

Half the harm that is done in this world is due to people who want
to feel important … They justify it because they are absorbed
in the endless struggle to think well of themselves.
—T. S. Eliot

Americans are experiencing an epidemic in narcissistic behavior in a culture
that is intrinsically self-conscious and selfish, and citizens are encouraged
to pursue happiness and instant gratification of their personal desires.
—Kilroy J. Oldster

Have this mind among yourselves, which is yours in Christ Jesus,
who, though he was in the form of God, did not count equality
with God a thing to be grasped, but emptied himself, by taking
the form of a servant, being born in the likeness of men.
—Paul the apostle

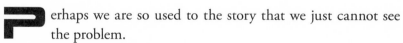

Perhaps we are so used to the story that we just cannot see
the problem.

The problem with us.

The problem with me.

We think we know and love Jesus. We listen to sermons, go to
classes, have devotional time in the Bible (maybe), and perhaps even
go really deep and attempt to write books about God.

But sometimes we just do not get Jesus.

We see him, if we care to, in numerous situations in which he is walking through life on earth as a pretty ordinary Jew. "He had no form or majesty that we should look at him, and no beauty that we should desire him."[105] He took on the role of a rabbi, or teacher, so he had a core group of learners (disciples) with him.

Just a pretty ordinary guy in a pretty ordinary place.

But ...

He was and *is* God. He is divine. He has the power to give life, restore life, or to destroy life with just a proclamation. He could defy the "laws" of nature, changing the molecular form of water into wine, walking on the water, and giving strength to legs that had never walked.

And yet,

> Have this in mind among yourselves, which is yours in Christ Jesus, who, though he was in the form of God, did not count equality with God a thing to be grasped, but emptied himself, by taking the form of a servant, being born in the likeness of men. And being found in human form, he humbled himself by becoming obedient to the point of death, even death on a cross.[106]

Do you get it?

The apostle Paul is inviting us to unpack *the attitude* we are to have as followers of the Christ. He wants us to see something and then make it true in our lives. It is absolutely stunning, breathtaking, and too often completely unheeded in our Christian lives today.

Emptying ourselves.

Truly serving, without making a big show of it.

Being truly humble, not drawing attention to what we have done or demanding that people recognize us as great, noble, or virtuous.

I've watched this phenomenon, the social media mission trip. A believer goes on a short-term trip, and the pictures and words follow.

The grueling airplane ride, the tired and sweaty face after a very long day in a hot climate, and the obligatory picture with a dark-skinned child—something even one Christian satire site made fun of because it is all so predictable and "look at me" centered.

Can I be your Dave? Can I be my Dave?

We can spiritualize this all day long, but can you be honest with yourself?

Would you even go on a short-term mission trip if no one knew you were doing it?

You see, we live in the age of the platformed self.

Previous generations would have called it self-idolatry or pride. Pride is not a good thing biblically, you know?

Have This Attitude

Back to the words of Paul the apostle we spoke of earlier.

That was only a sound bite of his complete statement. The letter of Philippians is known as the epistle of *joy,* but perhaps secondarily it should be known as the letter of humility.

Earlier in the chapter, from which we took the "have this mind" precept, he speaks of how living for Christ to advance the Gospel is his life, but dying and being with Christ would be even better.

What a joy that truly is—for it speaks the truth that for the believer who is obedient to God (a big *if* today), as we pursue kingdom objectives, we are in a win-win scenario. If we succeed in advancing the kingdom, we win. If someone kills us, we win!

But then he begins the line of thought that leads to the "have this mind" principle with the following: "Only let your manner of life be worthy of the gospel of Christ."[107]

Understand, the apostle is about to give us something that, if embraced, leads to a worthy manner of life. Let us see together what this worthiness looks like.

> So if there is any encouragement in Christ, any comfort from love, any participation in the Spirit, any affection and sympathy, complete my joy by being of the same mind, having the same love, being in full accord and of one mind.[108]

Stop there. Whatever it is that is the choosing of a worthy mindset and manner of life, it is something we are to do as *us!* This goes back to the "our, not my" principle of the earlier chapter. We as Christ's body are to embrace this *mind* together. Whatever he is going to instruct us to adopt as an attitude and action of the heart is something every believer is to adopt.

Are you ready for it?

> Do nothing from selfish ambition or conceit, but in humility count others more significant than yourselves. Let each of you look not only to his own interests, but also to the interests of others. Have this mind among yourselves, which is yours in Christ Jesus, who, though he was in the form of God, did not count equality with God a thing to be grasped, but emptied himself, by taking the form of a servant, being born in the likeness of men.[109]

Do nothing? I'm always intrigued and sit up straight when I find the inspired Word of God telling me to not do something, which is what this is. We are to be absolutely void of self-serving, self-promoting, image seeking (other than the image of Christ), popularity, trendiness, or appearing authentic.

Do *nothing* of that.

Can you be honest before God and yourself? Are you concerned with what others think of you and your apparent spirituality? Are you endeavoring to be a spiritual leader through making an impression on others of your spiritual wisdom, insight, and cleverness of speech?

If so, you have some work to do.

Ditch the cape.

And the superhero suit.

We are to be clothed in the righteousness of Jesus alone.

How do we purge our souls of a desire to be religiously respectable?

Interestingly, that is one of the topics Jesus himself dealt with in the Sermon on the Mount:

> Beware of practicing your righteousness before other people in order to be seen by them, for then you will have no reward from your Father who is in heaven.[110]

His answer to the problem, though, was *himself.* "Blessed are the poor in spirit, for theirs is the kingdom of heaven"[111] is not a command that we be self-deprecating; it was just a statement affirming to the people who had just witnessed him healing the sick. Because of Jesus, we who are with him are good to go. We need nothing—not the approval of men, not the praise of leaders, nor do we need title.

Being the child of God, the brother or sister of Jesus, and dressed in his righteousness alone—we have all we need.

Repent of your pride. Ditch the cape. Let Jesus be the star of the show.

Dave out …

SECTION II

The Antidote

SECTION II

Preface: Now for the Really Good Stuff!

My first officer and I were checking into our room at a rather nice hotel. It was 2022, and the policy at this hotel and city was masks recommended but optional. I and my working buddy were not masked. We were both believers, had examined the mortality rates of the disease, and had no fear of it.

As we finished our check-in, I saw a double-masked woman walking toward us from the left. She saw us without our masks and glared at me with her eyes, picked up her pace, and walked past us toward the elevator. She gave me a very direct stink-eye look as she walked right in front of me.

We received our key cards and followed her. As she reached the elevator, she went in an open one and glared back at me one more time. She seemed to be seething at us unmasked fellows. She had the posture of someone living in abject fear.

I put my hand out in front of my fellow pilot and quietly said, "Let's let her go alone. I don't think she wants to be around us."

The elevator door closed, and we waited. This hotel had the card scanner you had to use to get the elevator to go to a guest floor. The big annunciator over the door stayed on "1."

We waited, not wanting to push the button and make her any more scared or angry than she already was.

The elevator stayed on the first floor. My copilot looked at me quizzically and pointed toward the "up" button. I nodded. He pushed the button, the elevator reopened, and there was the woman curled up in a ball, crying on the floor.

I rushed in to her.

"Oh no! What's wrong, sweetie?"

"I can't get the elevator to move!" she stated, never looking up.

"Oh, that's okay. You just scan your room key and push the button," I assured her.

She began crying harder. "I don't have a room key. I'm just visiting my sister."

"No problem. I'll scan my key, and you can push the floor you want," I continued, trying to get her on her way.

She looked up, eyes full of tears, still on the floor in the back of the elevator. "Will you push the button for me?"

"Sure thing. What floor?"

"Four."

I scanned my card, pushed the button, and stepped out of the elevator. She finally moved upward. My copilot and I got the next elevator, also to the fourth floor, where our rooms were. As we arrived on the floor and turned down the hallway toward our rooms, there was our double-masked lady again—head bowed, crying loudly.

I walked up beside her and gently touched her back. "Oh no. What's wrong?"

"I'm on the wrong floor!" she said, and started crying even more hopelessly.

I patted her back softly and said quietly, "Hey, we're in this together. Let's go back to the elevator and get you on your way to the right place."

She looked up at me. "You would do that for me?"

"Yes, we are all in this life together. We have to stick together and help each other."

She stared into my eyes for a moment and then said, "You're a lovely human!"

"Aww, you're sweet!" I replied, and I walked her back and helped her on her way.

Child of the Delusion

This sweet lady was just one example of a child of the mass delusion. She is lonely, isolated, terrified, angry, and on the verge of curling up into a ball at any moment.

She had been told of her enemy—the unmasked. The unmasked was very likely a conservative, heteronormative, cisgender white male, an intolerant and abusive person who should not be allowed to exist. Because of the inherent evil of such an identity, as I represented to her, I was the reason for her suffering. My not wearing a mask was an attempt to harm her in her double-masked, likely double-vaccinated state (with a booster or two on board?).

Oh yeah, she probably suspected which presidential candidate I had voted for as well.

And so she hated me from the moment she saw my unmasked face.

But of course, I'm a dead man walking. I have the good news—no, I have the *great news*. I know the Christ. There is no need to be isolated. He died to establish his family on earth. We are admonished through his Word to do all of these "to one another's," well, *to one another!* I am continually surrounded by wonderful people who love and care for me.

I have purpose. In fact, in that moment when she was curled up in the elevator, my purpose was to slosh some of the love of her Creator onto her. After all, he had coated me in his love for decades. I always have extra!

Furthermore, I have power—but it is him working through me for his purposes. I am not at all like some powerful people who use intimidation, manipulation, or physical strength to use others for what I want. No, the power that flows through me can only work beautiful and loving purposes in accordance with the heart of God.

I have a peace that surpasses understanding. Anyone can experience a momentary peace when things are going our way. But to be able to stand in the strongest of storms and say nothing more to Yeshua the Messiah than "I trust you" is a very attractive quality to those who only get the briefest glimpses of peace.

When it comes to anger, there is a righteous anger. When people harm other people or take advantage of them, we have a specific anger at the injustice of that. That comes from the heart of God. We do not have a nonspecific anger because of some feeling of being out of control; we understand that we do not have control. We are the children of the one who controls all.

Though this precious lady started off our public interaction glaring and trying to let me know that I was her enemy, I did not respond in kind. Because I am just a grape branch, dwelling firmly grafted into the master vine, what flowed through me from our Lord was mercy, love, and grace.

It was nothing good of me; it was the good of the one in whom I dwell and who dwells in me.[112]

Our position is the strongest. We have the antidote to the current mass delusion. The faith we pursue as followers of *the way* is beautiful when lived boldly, but we must live boldly!

Bold Stuff—Live Out Loud

In this section, we will *celebrate* the characteristics of life in Christ that counteract all the current destructive characteristics of our imploding society. We need a reminder of the beauty that is produced when we dwell as members of the household of God, allowing our Lord to work his power through us—to tear down the work of his enemy's hands.

This may require us to change the way we approach church, but it is absolutely essential to be the bride (church) God intended. We will look at the beauty of what our Lord offers to us and do some strong thinking about the beam in our eye, so that we can help with that speck in the eye of the unbeliever.

We have the strongest position of hope, love, grace, and mercy of anybody in the world. We just need to see it with fresh eyes.

If we do that, his bride will become captivating to a lost and hopeless world.

Let's do this ...

CHAPTER 10

The Ultimate Life-Giving Connection

Solitude vivifies; isolation kills.
—Joseph Roux

The worst cruelty that can be inflicted on a human being is isolation.
—Sukarno

Too much self-centered attitude, you see, brings, you see, isolation. Result: loneliness, fear, anger. The extreme self-centered attitude is the source of suffering.
—Dalai Lama

Isolation is the sum total of wretchedness to a man.
—Thomas Carlyle

Bear one another's burdens and so fulfill the law of Christ.
—Paul the apostle

~~~~~~

Suicide patrol. That's what I did.

In the Second Gulf War, while stationed in the United Arab Emirates, I spent my off days walking around our encampment looking for people who were off to themselves. It's not that the war was so terrible that people couldn't bear living; it's just that we were living in a brown desert in brown tents. We were isolated from our normal groups of friends and family back home. The war was pretty political and stupid on our end. Most of our missions were just an attempt to keep the mission rate high so someone could get decorated or promoted. We flew empty airplanes all over Iraq and Afghanistan, every day. We got shot at flying empty airplanes to get our leadership team some nice Bronze Star medals and promotions.

It was a lovely, stupid, and meaningless mission.

Isolated people without a true purpose tend to lose perspective, get depressed, and sometimes attempt suicide.

A few other officers and I just decided to walk about and engage isolated people. Although suicides were on the rise in 2004 in the combat zone, fortunately we experienced none at our base.

The Combat Zone around You

Spiritual warfare is raging all around you. We need to join the fight for what is good and right to the glory of our great Lord and Savior.

One survey of American adults showed 36 percent of them experiencing feelings of loneliness "frequently" or "almost all the time."[113] If this rate holds true for the entire population, that would mean that in your life, more than one-third of all your neighbors, coworkers, and the people you walk next to in your town are *very lonely*. Possibly more than half of all people are thus lonely at some level, even though they are surrounded by neighbors, coworkers, and family.

Even sadder, this trend is hitting young adults (61 percent[114]) hardest, and mothers with young children (51 percent[115]) are struggling as well.

Further, as you might have suspected, nearly half of young adults reported that their loneliness has increased since the pandemic (43 percent[116]). This same demographic also is experiencing high rates of anxiety and depression.[117]

Yet those of us who are in Christ and who have "redemption

through his blood, the forgiveness of our trespasses, according to the riches of his grace, which he lavished upon us"[118] can rejoice that we do not suffer the same.

Or do we?

Can I be your Dave, church?

I don't have statistics for this—it is just an experiential impression—but we in the church are not much different in this loneliness, depression, and anxiety area. The sheer number of believers I know personally who cannot cope with life without drugs, overeating, or other comforting addictions tells me that the peace that our Lord promised us has not been received in any large measure by churchgoers today.

This. Must. Change.

When we consider all of those *to one another* admonishments and the impact they would have in anyone's life if embraced, we can see where the problems lie in the American church today. We can see, let the reader understand, the *beam* that is in our own eye.[119]

A friend who had been living in the Washington, DC, area moved back to the so-called Bible Belt where I live. We think of ourselves as being more religious, more engaged, and perhaps more authentic than those believers in the North, where there are fewer churches and they are frequently smaller.

My friend shared with me his concern when he moved back to the town where I live and began worshipping in our large church. "The church up there gets together a whole lot more than you guys here do."

That is pretty sad, and it is also unbiblical. It's one thing to show up in a pew a time or two every week and get outwardly excited (or not) and call ourselves *church members.*

But recognize that the early church met "every day, in the temple and from house to house."[120] There is no indication that this was some formal, big church event with lights, smoke, and a latte-drinking, trendy pastor making some big production for an audience.

No, it was the "our, not my" group of blood-bought believers pulling together because they needed one another. They were taking seriously the recent words of the apostles to love one another, and they were seeking to glorify Christ in all that they did—so they just kept getting together, especially in homes.

They were trying to grow and carry out their New Covenant mission. They needed one another and enjoyed the encouragement, support, love, and even the rebuke they received by spending lots of time together. They were fighting for the cause of the Christ and his beautiful mission of reconciliation, fighting for one another (through the "to one another's"), and standing side by side in close battle formation.

There was persecution. It could be dangerous.

It was dangerous. People died for their faith.

The church was thriving.

Bear, Share, Care, and Stop Hiding

> Brothers, if anyone is caught in any transgression,
> you who are spiritual should restore him in a spirit
> of gentleness. Keep watch on yourself, lest you too
> be tempted. Bear one another's burdens, and so
> fulfill the law of Christ.[121]

This instruction to the new church at Galatians says much. First, it acknowledges the everyday struggle of life, that people— even God's people (or *especially* God's people?)—are going to make a mess of things sometimes. The church has her orders. The "our, not my" are to gently surround the person struggling with sin and pull them back to the light.

We are to care, to have a compassionate spirit for our people who have given into the animalistic side of our being—and draw them in love back to the spiritual side of life. And those same people who are struggling are to care for me and you, as we are cut from the same cloth. I may appear strong today, but hang with me a week or two. I'll need you to rebuke, encourage, and love me shortly.

This requires, on the part of all of us, a refusal to wear a mask. We live in a strange time in which the word *authentic* gets thrown around, yet we actually are not talking about true authenticity.

We instead are emphasizing an *appearance* of realness, looking grungy, embracing sinful living, and being trendy. It is seen as brave to dress in a manner that defies social norms or to *come out* as a sinner and proudly expect everyone to cheer you on.

That is not the way of the Christ:

> Do nothing from selfish ambition or conceit, but in humility count others more significant than yourselves. Let each of you look not only to his own interests, but also to the interests of others. Have this mind among yourselves, which is yours in Christ Jesus, who, though he was in the form of God, did not county equality with God a thing to be grasped, but emptied himself, by taking the form of a servant, being born in the likeness of men. And being found in human form, he humbled himself by becoming obedient to the point of death, even death on a cross.[122]

Being Christlike is the antithesis of striving to *appear* to be authentic. It is instead a heart attitude that strives to reject *appearing* to be anything and is willing to accept anonymity in all things. The ecclesia, properly understood, is the land of the dead.

When we come to Christ, we undergo a symbolic death to self. As one writer put it,

> I have been crucified with Christ. It is no longer I who live but Christ who lives in me.[123]

Dead people do not worry about appearing to be anything. Neither should we, for it is a fool's errand. It doesn't matter what you think about how authentically spiritual and bold I am if my Lord knows I am a cowardly fraud!

Pretending to be someone you are not keeps others, by necessity, at arm's length. There can be no intimacy, no burden bearing, and no true *to one another love* if we are posturing in a vain attempt to appear to be what we are not.

The church of the dead is the most gritty, real, and engaging place of acceptance in the world. It is a people worth dying for.

Sebastian Junger, in his important work *Tribe: On Homecoming and Belonging,*[124] notes the following about truly authentic and thriving community:

> The earliest and most basic definition of community—of tribe—would be the groups of people that you would both help feed and help defend. A society that doesn't offer its members the chance to act selflessly in these ways isn't a society in any tribal sense of the word; it's just a political entity that, lacking enemies, will probably fall apart on its own.

"Will probably fall apart on its own."

Those words resonated with me when I first read his book just a few months ago. I had been sitting with my church one Sunday night, observing the backs of the heads of the people sitting in front of me. "We're getting old—we're dying" were the words that came to me. We as a family had identified a decade earlier that there was a particular demographic missing from our ecclesia—the twenty-five- to thirty-five-year-olds. While it is popular among older churchgoers such as myself to criticize younger generations, in truth, it just doesn't fly.

Every generation has its unique outlook and challenges regarding life. The good news of the Christ has eternal appeal. If a certain group doesn't participate in my church, then we in the church are likely the issue. We are fulfilling Junger's description of a group "that doesn't offer its members the chance to act selflessly in these ways isn't a society."[125] Thus our family is "falling apart on its own."

My church does a lot of good things, but too many of us hardly know each other. We live the classic American isolated life. We go to our comfy homes and sit in front of the big-screen TV or bow our head reverently before the almighty smartphone. We *amuse* ourselves. The root words of *amuse* are "a," which means *without,* and *muse* or "the mind." We spend so much of our time with our mind idling. Did not Jesus admonish us to love the Lord *with all our mind?* Instead, we imbibe the comforts and thrills of dopamine and take up our precious life with activities unworthy of our time.

Churches over the past several decades, as mentioned earlier, have drawn (or attempted to draw) numbers into the building through being seeker sensitive. We tell people how belonging will improve their lives. "We have youth ministry, young singles, marriage, and moms with preschoolers' ministries," we say as we try to sell a membership to our church.

Dietrich Bonhoeffer correctly presented another angle on church: "When Christ calls a man, he bids him come and die."[126]

Which message to the seeker should we be presenting?

Becoming Church

One of the exciting things going on in my community was started by a wonderful, neat guy in my church family. He has invited a bunch of us to join him, and it is just getting off the ground as I write this.

He calls it *The Daily Good.*

"Why is God's love for me so hard to accept?" was the question he asked me at one point. He accepts it now, with tears of joy. And he wants to slosh that love on others.

He is a home builder, and our community is beginning to experience a lot of homelessness or people whose homes are in very bad shape—and they cannot afford to fix them. He is organizing groups of believers and nonbelievers to get together and help. He schedules workdays to do something like a two-day renovation on a single mom's house. A large crowd of people come together for that time and work shoulder to shoulder, talk, share, and struggle to repair the house and make it clean and safe to live in.

Isn't that nice?

Well maybe, but you should see what it does for those of us on the work crew. Strong connections are formed. Social levels of rich or poor are meaningless. Everyone just stands and works together to help someone who really needs help.

Many in the community notice and don't get it. In a selfish society, why would you put your time and money to help someone you don't know, who perhaps has made some really bad decisions that led to them being where they are—and who can do nothing in return?

That's an awkward question, but isn't that what Jesus did for each of us?

> God shows his love for us in that while we were still sinners, Christ died for us.[127]

The *why* of Jesus doing what he did for us is the very thing that started my friend's heart churning to be Christlike to the hurting and hopeless of our town. Jesus's love doesn't make sense from a purely human perspective. The actions of my friend and the people he organizes to help others seem superheroic to those on the outside.

And then, to those on the outside, you see an amazingly diverse group of people connected to one another and enjoying the work. For those who are lonely, is this not a draw?

Closer Than a Brother?

The loneliness of younger people was confusing to me. I work with young people quite a bit, and they seemed well connected. On the other hand, the rates of loneliness, depression, substance abuse, and self-harm is rising at an alarming rate.

Simon Sinek noted in an interview that there has been a social media / smartphone–related factor in the shallowness of the social bonds formed today (and likely, not just for the young). Young people are often seemingly surrounded by friends, but these relationships are different from the friendships of pre-smartphone times and of the Bible:

> A man of many companions may come to ruin, but
> there is a friend who sticks closer than a brother.[128]

This proverb powerfully describes what is going on today. The idea of having a few friends who stick by your side, even closer than a blood relative, is obviously very attractive. To know that you have a few people in your life who would never abandon you and would always come to your aid seems too good to be true.

Back to the Simon Sinek interview. What he noted was that for many wonderful young people today, there is a problem in the nature of their friendships. Although they appear to have a lot of friends, there is a lack of depth and trust to these friendships. The impact of our social media culture is seen here.

The big concern developed through social media is that one be liked, admired, and *look* good. *Authenticity* is one of the buzzwords. This produces in social media–active individuals a desire to be seen by all as capable, successful, and together. The actual in-person friendships apparently are not immune to this. While young people (including young adults) may have many friends, there is a lack of depth, trust, and authenticity in these relationships.

When things go bad for someone with these superficial-level

friendships, they obviously cannot go to their friends, for that would spoil the perfect and *likeable* image that they have become accustomed to presenting.

So they do not ask for help from friends. They go to their phones. They *might,* if they have the resources, go to a professional counselor. This is better than a phone (perhaps), although generally not necessarily.

Having gone through the training to be a marriage and family therapist, I can say that much of what I do to help others is nothing more than what the "to one another" admonishments in the Word commend. Most therapy sessions are just a matter of listening closely, asking good questions, and coming alongside another person to help them process a tough situation.

There's nothing magic about therapy. What most of us really need to solve our worst problems is caring connection. This requires trust, love, and a commitment to stay with.

What we all need to deal with the tough side of life is someone *closer than a brother.*

Or perhaps, a whole crazy bunch of people who love you no matter what—in other words, the family of weirdos we call church. Let's look at how beautiful those "to one anothers" can be, just considering four of them.

Life Like This? Wow!

1.   *Love one another with brotherly affection (Romans 12:10).* I don't know if you have a church family, but I have several. Whenever I get together with any of these folks, I get mobbed with hugs, pats on the back, and incredible words of encouragement. The word underlying "brotherly affection" is the same root as *Philadelphia.*

It's all about brotherly love (or "sisterly" if you prefer). This invokes principles of kindness, warm affection, and care. This doesn't occur in a time-sensitive mass of people sitting in an auditorium.

It takes some face-to-face time. It requires conversation, listening, and reflecting together.

2.   *Outdo one another in showing honor (Romans 12:10).* What a beautiful concept. This word *honor* involves value, esteem, and dignity. God's people, his church, are to attempt to outdo one another in showing this *to one another!* Is this what your church is doing? Is this what *you* are doing to others in your church family?

Showing honor to others is much easier if you are comfortable in your own skin. This is what this book is all about, being who God says you are. If you are unconcerned with what others think of you because you have chosen to embrace what God says about you, then you can easily honor others because they are made in the image of God.

3.   *Live in harmony with one another. Do not be haughty, but associate with the lowly (Romans 12:16).* Do not make the mistake of thinking that harmony just happens. The Greek words underlying this term indicate a *setting of the mind, a choice,* to live in grace-filled and peaceful way. This require humility, knowing that we may be wrong in our strongly held doctrinal beliefs. As the passage notes, there is no room for a haughty spirit.

4.   *Bear one another's burdens, and so fulfill the law of Christ (Galatians 6:2).* The last few weeks have been a challenge. I lost two friends, one to suicide and another in a helicopter crash. My uncle died following a difficult time of illness. I had a conflict over some traditions at church, which were resolved (I think) only through some very challenging conversations.

But my church family was praying for me, taking me out to eat, and surrounding me with love and supportive words. It was doable. The called out of God came to my side. I can't imagine how hard this would have been without the anti-isolation of God's big family.

We all need help with the burdens of life. The church was intended to meet that need.

The Challenge for Loving the Isolated

If you think about the way many of the unchurched are so isolated, and further, may not be too good at making connections, then the question becomes, *how do we pull someone into the household of God to begin with?*

Particularly, if you are part of a large, building-centric church, is a somewhat socially awkward, isolated person just going to waltz into your service and make themselves at home?

Not likely, is it?

We will talk more about the specifics of this later in section III, but the best way to bring someone into our church family is to *bring them.* This presupposes that you build a friendship with them and insistently ask them to come to activities (not just or necessarily worship) of your church family. You can bring them to small group, cookouts, service projects, and of course times of worship. All the while, if your church has the eyes of Christ and his love is flowing through them, they will find something very remarkable in the process: they will feel loved.

Let's face it. Going to church, as in walking into a church service, when you are not used to it can be a pretty weird and seemingly unnatural experience. We have our own language of sorts, we stand and raise hands (or not!), we sing together (not necessarily what the unchurched are used to, and many people are self-conscious about singing in public), and some of our churches feature some strange-looking costumes (vestments and the like). Instead of trying to coax people into a building, what if we just bring our new friends side by side and guide them through the "strangeness."

Part of this challenge remains the same regardless. If we are to provide the anti-isolation antidote to this current crisis of mass delusion, we in the local church family must overcome our fear of rejection and be friendly. We must reach out in a natural way (not in the creepy "everyone stand up and greet the person next to you" deal) so that the church becomes what it is supposed to be—a place where everyone is welcomed because our Creator wants his creation gathered.

If you aren't good at initiating and sustaining conversation with someone you do not know, we'll cover the basics of how to learn that in section III. Or perhaps your little God family can do some training on this.

But especially in a large church, we need to have a natural and familial way of recognizing that someone is new and a comfortable and loving way of approaching them. I suppose greeters are okay, but what if everyone was on the lookout for everyone? I know that in our building, most of us sit in about the same place every week. This is one good way for a member to stake a claim and look for new faces in their immediate area. If someone new does show up, they can meet them, start a friendship (this isn't hard; it is a learned ability), and take the opportunity to connect the visitor (especially if they are local) with some other members who have similar interests.

As someone who travels for a living, I've walked into a lot of churches, and I must say, the ones where someone just approaches you like they are already your friend and then insists that you either stay to eat (if there is a church meal that day) or that you come home or go out to eat with them are the best! In my line of work, the weekend layovers are long and lonely. I appreciate, even as a believer, being included in the special times of sharing a meal.

I recommend that we change our view of bringing or welcoming visitors from a mission of "raising attendance" to one of "making a friend and sharing the love of God." The Bible is specific about God bringing about growth. If we will just be a friend to those we meet, like Jesus was, we can stop treating people like projects and instead just enjoy the friend-making process.

Being the "our, not my" family of God is indeed the anti-isolation solution. Note that this requires us to be together a whole lot more than just for something we might call formal worship. Scripture notes that the early church met "every day, in the temple and from house to house,"[129] and while that is nothing binding on us, it is instructive.

We need to avoid isolation. Being with people is far superior to cocooning in our homes in front of an HDTV or bowing before our screens. We must choose to be with people and to truly and honestly share our lives together.

Church was and is the life-giving connection our Creator knew we must have to thrive. Humans suffer when the church fails to be the place where people gather, belong, and embrace the "to one anothers."

Dave out ...

CHAPTER 11

The Life-Giving Mission of the Living Dead

The typical modern has the look of the hunted.
—Richard M. Weaver

A person without a purpose is a human being merely breathing because he does not know where he is, let alone knowing where he is going. Purposelessness is lifelessness.
—Israelmore Ayivor

The LORD will fulfill his purpose for me; your steadfast love, O LORD, endures forever. Do not forsake the work of your hands.
—King David

large percentage of those around us see very little meaning to life. They perceive that their lives do not matter and that they have very little control over what happens to them or around them. This lack of meaning making is another factor in the process of mass delusion that produces atrocities.

The ecclesia, the body of Christ, the disciples—a.k.a. the church—is the perfect antidote to anyone perceiving that their life lacks purpose. It is also the conduit of power to the powerless. If you are a follower of the way, you may not be experiencing this intense and always present purpose.

Nor may you feel powerful.

Can I be your Dave? If your life as a blood-bought believer is not intensely and continually purposeful and filled with power, you are doing church life wrong. Let us look together at the life-giving and consuming mission of the body of Christ.

Sufficient Ministers of a New Covenant

We, as blood-bought believers, have been given a tremendous gift. When we come into a vibrant faith in Christ, it isn't just to save our skin from burning in hell.

No, a faith in Christ isn't just for selfish, self-serving motives.

The apostle Paul makes it clear in various parts of his writing that something incredibly significant happened to us, things that we should have agreed to, when we put on Christ in baptism. It starts in the book of Romans with one of his typical "Do you not know" questions:

> Do you not know that all of us who have been baptized into Christ were baptized into death, in order that, just as Christ was raised from the dead by the glory of the Father, we too might walk in newness of life.[130]

And thus, the old Pharisee lets us know that we are with him. After his baptism, he was no longer Saul the rising Pharisee; he was something completely new. Not just someone new but *something* new—a new creature with a new purpose.

It is therefore true that we do not share the world's despair in living a life without meaning, impact, or purpose. We do not sleepwalk through the days, just living for our next hit of dopamine or hoping someone will think we are somebody when we are not. The living dead just have no desire for that.

Ours is a glorious and exciting purpose, a mission to be engaged in nearly every aspect of life—all of life except perhaps in our incidental physiological functions.

Are we on mission?

Can we voice our mission?

We return to the writings of the former Pharisee ("phormer Pharisee?") to see the most complete explanation of what gives us purpose in every moment of wherever our Lord has placed us.

> Our sufficiency is from God, *who has made us sufficient to be ministers of a new covenant,* not of the letter but of the Spirit. For the letter kills, but the Spirit gives life ... if there was glory in the ministry of condemnation, the ministry of righteousness must far exceed it in glory ... since we have such a hope, we are very bold ... Now the Lord is Spirit, and where the Spirit of the Lord is, there is freedom. And we all, with unveiled face, beholding the glory of the Lord, are being transformed into the same image from one degree of glory to another. For this comes from the Lord who is the Spirit.[131]

Can you sense the thrill and excitement of Paul? He cannot seem to find sufficient praise or description of the glorious nature of the mission we have been given as *the living dead.* He's just getting rolling. Paul is filled with amazing joy at the beautiful purpose that has become his life. We share in this purpose—if we name the Christ as Lord! Let us look together at a few of the jewels of our ministry in Him that fill every day with purpose.

Precept #1: Therefore, knowing the fear of the Lord, we persuade others.[132]

The fear of the Lord is the beginning of wisdom. The reaction of anyone who experiences even a portion of the glory of God in scripture is to collapse and hide their faces in the dust. To just begin to grasp the greatness and complete otherness of our Creator God is overwhelming beyond description. Fear is a starting point.

Because of this reality, we see the proud unbeliever with compassion, for we know that they need to know the overwhelming nature of that glory before it is experienced too late. We can stand in the freedom our loving Creator gave us on earth and doubt, blaspheme, and malign the name of God, but the day is coming for us all when we will experience the Dread Sovereign Lord of the universe in all of his fullness. For those in rebellion to him, it will be a horrific and terrifying day. There will be no proud faces or taunting challenges raised to the Sovereign of the universe. Therefore:

Purpose #1: Because we have experienced a portion of the unfathomable glory of God and the resultant fear, we must warn those who do not know him before it is eternally too late.

Every person we meet, work with, or stumble across must be seen potentially as a divine appointment. It's not that we have to convert every unbeliever on the spot, but we are to be *light* to a person who is dwelling in the darkness of alienation from their loving Father.

Every moment with others has purpose. Every home of a believer, whether an ornate and stately home or a packing crate home in a homeless camp, is a strategic outpost from whence the beautiful light of our Savior is to shine.

Application #1: Wherever you work, live, or go, prayerfully and boldly look for our divine appointment of the moment.

Whether you are a homemaker or businessman, whether you live in the inner city or out in the country, God hasn't made a mistake in where he has placed you. You are on mission right where you are.

Author Rosaria Butterfield answered a question from a somewhat different neighbor as to why she was friends with him, given his unusualness. Her answer was "Because God never gets the address wrong."[133]

While she advocates for a powerful form of spiritual warfare in our homes through seeing our street address as something God intended, I contend this principle applies to all of life.

Yes, your house, apartment, condo, tent, or any dwelling is *the* place where God placed you—for the purpose of sharing his love and fighting back the darkness of evil.

So is your workplace. Whether that is a corporate boardroom, a big-box store, a classroom, or at home raising children, *your* mission from God is where he has placed you, now.

As you walk through the day at work, allow the Holy Spirit to direct your attention to those he is working on. At one point in my airline job, I made a vow with God to ask everyone I flew with in a particular month if they had any spiritual beliefs. It was an amazing month.

Every single person I asked was in the middle of a spiritual search or struggle! The Spirit was already working on these hearts; all I had to do was join in his work in the time that I had with them.

Divine appointments. They are awesome. They are the reason that as of the writing of this book, I have not yet retired. I get excited about what God is going to be doing in the lives of the people he places me with. I get to come alongside him and join him in his beautiful work of reconciliation.

Divine appointments occur in the routine and boring errands of life too. Just going to town to get the list done, I have encountered people in whose life God was working. People who were hurting and scared, God placed me in their path for a bit of love, encouragement, and friendship. I rarely am the closer. I usually do not see the end of the work he is doing, but I have seen it enough to trust and understand that I just need to have my eyes open and be faithful to love in that moment when the divine appointment happens.

Precept #2: "He died for all, that those who live might no longer live for themselves but for him who for their sake died and was raised."[134]

This is surely some strange good news, but it is actually great and healthy news. Once we are dead and raised as a new creature, we can ditch all the worries about *what's in it for me!* Our society is far more narcissistic than ever, and we are also far more suicidal than ever. The two are connected. The person wrapped up in themselves is the smallest and most miserable package around.

As we come to Christ and we see him on the cross, and we walk from there and peer into the tomb, finding it still empty, there is a message. Jesus is in effect saying, "You're good. Now go tell others they can have the same grace, mercy, love, and hope!"

What Joshua (a.k.a. Jesus) of Nazareth literally said was, "No one can serve two masters."[135] He is not commanding us to *not* serve two masters; he is just speaking a truth.

You cannot serve *you* and him.

But if you die to yourself and serve him, he will take care of you. No worries.

Thus the reason he calls us to die. Baptism—a way in which he demonstrates a type of death, burial, and resurrection—teaches our hearts something important. This event in our lives begins chipping away at our self-idolatry of attempting to serve ourselves (while pronouncing God's will on our selfishness) and claiming to be "in Christ."

He clarifies our mission just shortly after the statement above, in case we were unclear on how this was to look in our life:

> Seek first the kingdom of God and his righteousness,
> and all these things will be added to you.[136]

One of the surest ways to break free from depression is to have a purpose in life that breaks one out of the continual concern for one's own well-being. Knowing that you are connected with others for good, that you are needed in the world, and that everyone you meet is potentially someone you can help and can help you brings an excitement to even the worst encounters.

Knowing as well that we do not have to be concerned with our daily needs, but that God will give us what we need if we pursue what is on his heart, is also freeing. Living for others, while trusting our care to the Lord, who promises to give us what we need, is the surest path to an anxiety-free life.

Purpose #2: Because of the gift of grace lavished upon us, we no longer are focused on our success, our fame, our happiness, or our acceptance. Our focus and purpose is in sharing the glorious grace in which we stand. It is the ultimate freedom.

The blood-bought believer has no need to attempt to appear to be authentic or to be concerned about what someone thinks. Their worth, acceptance, and daily agenda have been determined by their joy in Christ.

This obviously is not an easy thing. But it is worthwhile.

"Why is accepting Jesus's love for me so difficult?" a new friend asked of me.

That is a great question. It is a struggle I would think most of us have. We struggle with the love of Christ and our worth being found in him because his love is so otherworldly. It took me more than a decade of scriptural study and contemplation, combined with a daily observant walk with God, to be convinced of the truth that God is crazy about crazy me.

Sometimes I really could not stand me, so how could God?

He convinced me.

In order to accept what Jesus speaks to you of your worth, beauty, and acceptance, you must take time to sit with him daily and share your heart. He shares his heart first through his Word, then through his church (the "our, not my"), and then throughout our day as he orchestrates events around us in his kingdom.

In my case, being raised in a religious tradition that strongly emphasized saving yourself through compliance with commands, it was difficult to even perceive and acknowledge that God was active and present in my daily life.

Yet the words of Paul in this section of the Bible about the new covenant are vital:

> Our sufficiency is from God, who has made us sufficient to be ministers of a new covenant, not of the letter but of the Spirit. For the letter kills, but the Spirit gives life.[137]

Our purpose is empowered by our walking in the Spirit and accepting our worth and identity *in Christ*. As we mature spiritually, the old concerns of "what do they think of me" fade, and our concern becomes "what does God want for *them*?" It is a beautiful life when we as his people can be comfortable in our own skin because we know we are loved, indwelt, and secure.

Application #2: Grow in the confidence of your worth, purpose, and provision in our Lord. Trust that he will give you all you need generously as you love others for his purposes.

Precept #3: We regard no one according to the flesh.[138]

Our Lord was countercultural in his day. He remains so to this very day. While many, even some believers, are claiming that your identity group is critical, the Gospel proclaims that the only identity that matters is the image of God in each and every person. Race, sex, whether or not you have been oppressed, and your favored chosen sin do not determine our regard.

Purpose #3: We refuse to participate in divisions according to the flesh. We accept only that the Creator made male and female, young and old,

*and that we have differing roles in the family and church but are all
equal as image bearers before our loving God. We love all and accept
all as we strive to be transformed from our sinful flesh to walk in the
Spirit through the power God provides.*

It is time to end the "race." God did not create races of people.
In the original garden, there were two persons, one man and one
woman. From them, all families of the world came to be. Not races,
families.

Further, I noticed in my own church that we have some very
fine (and truthful) sermons on the truth of the "one man"[139] origin
of us all. God designed within us the adaptability that allows our
bodies to adapt to whatever earthly environment we find ourselves
in for long. But there was a single origin family; therefore, we are all
ultimately of one family.

For that matter, the genetic tree branches out from Noah and
the three sons who were on the ark during the flood.

We are, as we like to say in the South, "cuzzes" (cousins).

We who know the Creator must treat all of our cousins with
love and not embrace a flesh-based error based upon recessive or
dominant genetic traits. We must also reject the currently popular
concept of *identifying* as something we cannot be. A man cannot
be a woman, even with the help of surgery and hormones. As
many feminists have pointed out, a man who has undergone sex
reassignment surgery is not a woman but a *man's idealized construct
of a woman.* A man surgically altered to appear thus did not carry
a uterus or the attendant female hormones as he grew. He did not
suddenly start bleeding at an embarrassing time and place. He did
not get the warning of how certain activities during a date could lead
to him blowing up like a balloon and having to change his entire
life to care for the child.

A surgically altered man has no concept of what being a woman
is. He is merely someone with a mental challenge that he has chosen
to cope with poorly. We must love such people. It is not loving to

encourage someone to exacerbate the problem by attempting to be something they can never be.

In sum, we can accept and love those with challenges. We should never encourage them to dive more deeply into their serious mental issues and embrace something that simply cannot be.

In other words, if we do regard them according to the sins or external properties of the flesh, we are violating who we are to be in Christ.

We are to see them as fallen image bearers of God—just as we are.

Application #3: Approach people as Jesus did. Love, compassion, and understanding are the foundations of friendship. Enabling the flesh destroys. We meet people where they are and point them toward Yeshua the Christ. And as he did, we accept and love them where they are, and we encourage them to repent and move toward what they were created to be.

The only thing that ultimately matters is that each person bears the image of God, and if they are not in a saving relationship with Jesus, then our loving priority is to endeavor to share the good news with them and accomplish the next aspect of the mission (or more accurately, allow God to work through us to accomplish this).

Precept #4: All this is from God, who through Christ reconciled us to himself and gave us the ministry of reconciliation; that is, in Christ God was reconciling the world to himself, not counting their transgressions against them, and entrusting to us the message of reconciliation.[140]

There have been times in my life where my wife and I got sideways with each other. They are very stressful and unhappy moments, but reconciliation is so sweet! To remove the barriers between each other and once again be one in spirit is purely awesome.

How much more so with our Lord! All of us have sinned and

fallen short of the glory of God. Our sin is reprehensible to him, and we cannot make it right in our own strength. So he had a plan.

In my church tradition, something is called the *plan of salvation*, and it is listed as steps, including the following:

1. Hearing the good news
2. Believing that Jesus is the Son of God
3. Repenting of your sins
4. Confessing Jesus as Lord and Savior
5. Being baptized for the remission of sins

While all of these items are found in scripture, they are *not* the plan of salvation. Yeshua the Messiah coming to earth as fully man, fully God, living for us and among us, and dying on the cross as an atoning sacrifice, and then demonstrating victory over death and reigning in heaven as Lord is the plan of salvation.

Those other items *are our response* to the plan; they need to happen.

But the plan is this person we usually call Jesus; his death, burial, and resurrection were vital for the plan. Through this, he reconciled "the world to himself, not counting their trespasses against them."[141] It is an amazing message and gift and the source of our hope!

Because of this, it has been entrusted "to us the message of reconciliation."[142] We stand every day and in every way as "ambassadors for Christ, God making his appeal through us," and if we are on mission, we become "the righteousness of God."[143]

This makes the kingdom of God and the "our, not my" family of God the source of the most important meaning in life that can be had—for in it is found the ultimate meaning: the spiritual life is the only enduring life there is.

Everything that we see around us is temporary; none of it will endure. It doesn't matter whether we as believers are rich or poor, beautiful or not, or eloquent or simple. If we are in Christ, we have within us the indwelling Spirit of God, and our purpose is the most beautiful and noble the world can know. The fact that we have the Holy Spirit endows us with power beyond human comprehension. When we look at the mess that is our world and feel overwhelmed and hopeless, we are right.

If it is up to us in our strength to fix it, we cannot and will not.

But if we, like the young shepherd boy David, come to the heat of the battle "in the name of the LORD of hosts,"[144] we can stand and watch as the Dread Sovereign Lord of Creation knocks down one giant threat after another before us. He does the work; we simply must stand in faith.

Our God, his great news (the Gospel), and his "our, not my" group of ragtag Spirit-empowered warriors are the ultimate weapon against a lack of meaning making in life. Our God can pull those poor souls out of their dark mass psychosis and delusion into the glorious light that is our Savior Yeshua of Nazareth, King of the universe, Lord of lords, and the Alpha and Omega.

Join the army of the living dead. It is a victory for all but Satan. Dave out …

CHAPTER 12

Free-Floating Shalom

Thou hast made us for thyself, O Lord, and our heart is restless
until it finds its rest in thee.
—Augustine of Hippo

A quiet conscience makes one strong!
—Aristotle

Peace I leave with you; my peace I give to you. Not as the world gives do
I give to you. Let not your hearts be troubled, neither let them be afraid.
—Yeshua the Messiah

〰〰〰〰〰〰〰〰〰〰〰〰〰〰〰〰〰〰

While those around us are experiencing free-floating anxiety, we have the ultimate antidote.

Free-floating shalom. Peace, love toward all, and an unconcern for our own status.

We have Yeshua the Messiah. We have his bride—one another, the "our, not my" band of loving family. We have the strongest gift to give humanity.

But I have to be completely honest about this topic. As I came to the writing of this chapter, I was stopped in my tracks. I was going through the most challenging time of my life. Peace was getting harder to find. The Lord sent me deeply into his Word, into prayer, into discussions with my brothers and sisters. It's one of the things I love about our Lord. His patience in teaching is abundant.

Our concept of *peace* in our times is sometimes shallow. It carries with it the concept of a lack of conflict, noise, or just a momentary sense of calm. Those things are certainly good—but when all around you is crumbling and noisy, how do you stand resolute?

But as we think about what we as the called out of Christ have to offer a desperate world, what Jesus showed us is far beyond just a respite from conflict or trouble.

Hebrew Peace, Greek Peace ...

The beautiful greeting of the family of Israel was *shalom*—a word rich in its beauty. It conveys a holistic sense of wellness, completeness, and joy.

One online word study noted that *shalom* "signifies a sense of well-being and harmony within and without—Completeness, wholeness, peace, health, welfare, soundness, tranquility, prosperity, fullness, rest, harmony; the absence of agitation or discord, a state of calm without anxiety or stress."[145]

That's a whole lot of blessing in a simple greeting—but of course it takes more than spoken words to produce that in our lives. Would it not be awesome to live our days in that level of complete peace?

When our Yeshua spoke of peace, sometimes he used the Greek term *eirene*. This word is underappreciated in a sense. It likely comes from the root word *eiro*, which curiously means "to join."

Join what?

I suppose that it signifies *wholeness* as opposed to division, but may I suggest that in the teachings of Jesus, there is another joining that is the path to a whole-person peace?

That is the question—and in the answer, we find how the *our, not my* called-out ones offer to a world full of anxiety a beautiful antidote to the free-floating anxiety that permeates society.

As to what we join, the clues to this beautiful process are found throughout the Word, starting with our Lord himself:

> Peace I leave with you; my peace I give to you. Not as the world gives do I give to you. Let not your hearts be troubled, neither let them be afraid.[146]

If he left this peace, how do we take hold of it? In this passage, he is speaking of his *leaving* and going to be with the Father once again. It was a very difficult time for his followers, many of whom conceived him to be an eventual earthly king—a misunderstanding still prevalent in some circles today.

But as you read on in this discussion the Messiah had with his followers, he gives the secret to receiving the peace of which he was speaking. You know that when people use repetition, they are trying to get us to understand something major. Look for the repeating word in the following words of Jesus (okay, so I italicized the repeating word in case you are sleepy):

> I am the true vine, and my Father is the vinedresser. Every branch in me that does not bear fruit he takes away, and every branch that does bear fruit he prunes, that it may bear more fruit. Already you are clean because of the word that I have spoken to you. *Abide* in me, *and I in you* as the branch cannot bear fruit by itself, unless it *abides* in the vine, neither can you, unless you *abide* in me. I am the vine; you are the branches. Whoever *abides* in me and I in him, he it is that bears much fruit, for apart from me you can do nothing. If anyone does not *abide* in me he is thrown away like a branch and withers; and the branches are gathered, thrown into the fire, and burned. If you *abide* in me, and my words *abide* in you, ask whatever you wish, and it will be done for

you. By this my Father is glorified, that you bear much fruit and so prove to be my disciples. As the Father has loved me, so I have loved you. *Abide* in my love. If you keep my commandments, you will *abide* in my love. These things I have spoken to you, that my joy may be in you, and that your joy may be full.[147]

Abide in me … the ultimate joining. He mentions this word or infers it at least ten times in this short passage! Yeshua the Messiah is inviting us to join with and in him—and from that joining, we receive a fullness of joy. Is not joy in Christ the foundation of peace?

It is my understanding from many years of a sometimes-faltering walk with the Lord that the only path to lasting peace is through abiding in Christ.

But can I honestly confess it is at times so gruelingly hard to do? At times, it has been unclear how to even abide at all!

Can I be *your* Dave (since I'm so busy being mine)?

In this section, we are discussing how the ecclesia should be the antidote to those elements of mass delusion that are leading our society toward great atrocities.

But does the "our, not my" church each of us is in exude this calm, whole, and joyful spirit that comes to those who are abiding in Christ? It is a question each of us and each of "our" needs to answer.

I would say in my knowledge of local congregations that God's children are doing substantially better than the average nonbeliever. The exciting and necessary thing is there is room for growth.

Think of it. How would each of us *share* the practical path to the shalom that is abiding in us? Let's look at that, and perhaps some of this will be helpful to you—as it has been and is to me.

The First Essential in the Path to Abiding (Shalom)

When I was thirty years old, I was going through an intense period of pursuing growth with God. I had been placed (by the Lord, I perceive) among a fantastic group of like-minded men. I confessed to them that I wanted to grow and be bold for God.

A couple of us went to a men's spiritual event. I needed encouragement and was eager to hear some of the speakers. The keynote speaker on the first day though was *just* a Baptist pastor from a large church in Memphis. I had never heard of him and did not have high hopes. I had heard a few Baptist pastors and had not been greatly moved. As he sat on the stage being introduced, I was even further disappointed; he *looked* boring.

His resting face looked dour, and his body and dress were, well, unimpressive? You can see how much growth I needed …

But he was the only option other than leaving the building for the next hour, so I settled in to endure this dreadful man and hopefully not snore.

The Dread Sovereign Lord of all the universe I suspect was snickering at me, if not engaged in a full-blown belly laugh, rolling on the golden floors of the throne room. He had set me up. His unimpressive man in the podium was about to skewer me with a Holy Spirit harpoon.

I was completely unsuspecting.

This man's topic, I wish I could remember his name, was growing spiritually—right up my alley? At one point, he launched the aforementioned harpoon, and it hit me dead center. I wish I had written down his words exactly, but at the moment the spear pierced my chest, I was unable to write or speak. It sunk deeply, it hurt, and it changed me forever.

The first essential step to *abiding* in Christ was revealed—and the reason why it was and continues to be was exposed to the glorious and painfully bright light of the Christ. He said something along the lines of the following, with a few of my thoughts interspersed:

177

"Every wife knows that her man will actually accomplish what he truly values in his heart, *to her pain.*"

I credit the Holy Spirit for the absolute immediacy of the quick recognition of what he had just said as being absolutely true not only of all men but of me specifically. In this one statement, I instantly saw through all of the feeble excuses I had given for the times I had failed to love my wife properly. It was because what I valued was not my vow to love her but rather that natural, fleshly tendency to make an idol of me.

The now not-so-boring-pastor continued: "If you are frustrated as a man because you are not where you say you want to be spiritually, it is because *you do not really want it. You are serving yourself, not God.*"

Harpoon number two hit its mark. I was at this conference because I claimed to wanted to grow spiritually. I had confessed that to my closest believing brothers. I assume they believed me. Heck, I believed me. But in this one moment with the "boring pastor," I was split open by the exposing of the true subject of my worship—me.

He and the Holy Spirit were not done with me yet: *"If you are not as close to God as you say you want to be, or used to be, you are the one who chose to move away. God will not ever leave you. If you feel distant from your Savior, you are the one who walked away."*

I was silenced, humbled, and crushed before God. My dishonesty with everyone, including myself, was peeled open—and the great mystery of why I was so *unspiritual* (witness my evaluation of the worth of this speaker based upon his physical appearance) was no longer a mystery.

Over the years, the Lord taught me some more about abiding in him, and in shalom, let me share a few principles with you.

Principles of abiding in Christ, of living in Shalom. If you want the peace of Christ, you must want Christ more than anything else. You must live out the covenant relationship you agreed to when you were baptized to *die* to yourself (baptism demonstrates the wisdom of God; it is a symbolic death and being raised to live to the purposes of our Savior) and to be engaged in an ongoing process of regeneration,[148] a process of becoming an entirely new person who lives abiding in the Christ each day. Practically, how do we make this happen?

1. *Embrace ceremonial grace.*

Much has been said on these topics over the years. Much division has resulted. I beg you to listen without prejudice and just consider the wisdom of God in the ceremony and symbolism he established and the benefit if confers to us.

Baptism by immersion in water has been a contentious topic for centuries now. Just speaking as your brother in the faith, it need not be.

Further, I want to make a case that we should value it far more than we have.

Case in point: I went through air force pilot training a few decades ago. It was a yearlong, very challenging course of training.

The stress is intense. You usually worked Monday through Friday with the weekends off, and we students often spoke of the "Sunday-night shakes." We enjoyed our weekends, but by Sunday night, we would find ourselves getting tense and anxious about what was about to start the following morning.

One day when I was in the advanced phase of training, I went to the men's room to, umm, take care of business. As I sat down in the stall, I noticed someone had written a message with a sharpie pen on the inside of the stall door: "Relax, this isn't graded! (It's the only thing!)"

I laughed out loud, but it was true. It seemed that you were continually being watched, inspected, and critiqued. It was a hard year. I sat in the stall and enjoyed the rare moment of unsupervised, umm, activity.

Interestingly, there comes a point where you have finished all the requirements to graduate. But you don't graduate.

For me, it was about three weeks before the program was over.

But I still had to show up every day and wear the uniform and participate in the ground training and social life of my class. I had done everything required to be an air force pilot in terms of practical training—but I was not yet an air force pilot.

You had to go through the pinning of your wings ceremony.

Pinning is fantastic. The air force brought in a distinguished, combat-proven general to speak and to personally give you your air force wings. My wife dressed up beautifully for the day, and my parents even flew in to be there. It was a celebration, it had very solemn moments, and much was made of the responsibility, benefits, and joy of wearing those wings.

At one point, my name was read. I walked up to the general and saluted him, and he returned my salute. He shook my hand and spoke great words of encouragement to a young man he didn't even know; he just knew that we now shared both the hard year of earning those wings, and now I would share the same journey of risk and joyous reward of wearing them.

We humans love ceremony. We celebrate graduations, engagements, promotions, marriage, the birth of children, holidays, and more. We humans *need* symbols and ceremony.

Three weeks before I got my wings, I had finished all the requirements of becoming an air force pilot, but I remained a *student*. Once the general handed me my wings, and then my beautiful wife who had immensely helped me make it through this tough year pinned them on me, I was now in. I then *and only then* became what I had wanted to be since the seventh grade.

I cried that day. I was amazed and thankful I had been able to do it. I felt accomplished.

I was changed.

I would wear those wings for two decades; they were a regular and encouraging reminder of who I was and what I had done.

Such is the power of ceremony.

As followers of Christ, we agree to join him in the New Covenant mission. How did we agree and become a party to that?

We died.

Yep, that is what the immersion under the water is supposed to symbolize for us. Our death and our being born again as a spiritual one-day old brother or sister to Yeshua, who is learning (being a disciple) to be on mission in his image every minute of every day.

I was only twelve when I was buried. I understood little. I mostly was afraid of hell. But as the psalmist notes, "The fear of the LORD is the beginning of wisdom."[149] I was at a beginning point of abiding in Christ, of finding peace.

Although I understood little and knew God barely, I still think back to that death—because it is a ceremony of enormous importance. It represents a change of who I was to be in every way for the rest of my life. Baptism is a physio-spiritual gift from God. It teaches our spirit through a physical and definite act that we went all-in when we voluntarily snuffed out our life. We should think of it often. It defines our transition as a reborn person in a definitive way.

Baptism is not a work. It physically accomplishes nothing.

It is a ceremony or a symbol through which we experience a defining point at which we ceased living for our self and sought to abide with Christ in the covenant.

Embrace the ceremonial grace of baptism.

2. *Make your daily time with the Lord an inviolate priority.*

Abiding in Christ requires we be in his presence. Acknowledging that our Lord is real and the center of our life requires us to prioritize sitting down with him daily and conversing.

The apostle Paul makes clear in the letter to the Ephesians that *marriage* is a symbol of the relationship between Christ and us, his ecclesia.[150] In working with married couples as well as in my own marriage, there has to be regular and open conversation. Couples who do not communicate drift apart; there is no true intimacy and togetherness without regular talk.

For me, meeting with our Lord first thing in the morning is essential and produces beautiful fruit. There is something about choosing to get a cup of coffee and just sitting down with our Savior and conversing that continually teaches my heart to *stay close to him throughout the day.* In other words, that disciplined habit of sitting with God and hearing from his Word and speaking with him solidifies our relationship.

It has to be regular though.

In many marriages, the man has a challenge in this area.

We men tend to be very task focused and linear in our pursuits. We will pay attention to our wives when we want something from them. If we get what we want, we move on.

Of course, our women are perceptive. They learn quickly when we do this that if we hubbies are being attentive, then there is a bill to be paid (let the reader understand!). That shuts down the relationship a bit, for instead of that attention being *love,* it is *manipulation.* It is *utilitarian.*

It is not good for the relationship.

If we only go to God to ask favors when we are in a bind, is that really abiding? Isn't that just like the husband who mainly pays attention to his wife when he wants sex? Isn't that manipulation and selfishness?

Back to the unimpressive Baptist pastor and the spiritual harpoons he pierced my sternum with. The *only sure way* we will know the peace of abiding in Christ is if we choose to stay close to him daily. We must always be seeking and sitting with him, walking with him, and talking with him.

Speaking of talking with him …

3. *Learn to pray without ceasing.*

Yep, 1 Thessalonians 1:17 is short and challenging: "Pray without ceasing."

As a kid, I just couldn't believe that was even in the Bible. How could someone sit with their head bowed speaking all those holy King James words all day long?

And therein lies a big part of the problem with our prayer life.

Too many of us learn to pray from listening to men who are either very nervous about praying in front of a crowd of people or who are trying to impress us with a flowery and pious-sounding prayer.

Let's cut to the chase here.

The Father God is our *Father.* Jesus instructed us to call him *Abba,* which is very much like the loving and familiar term *daddy* that many of us in the South used with our fathers.

I think back to raising my children when they were small. One of the refreshing (or alternatively, annoying) things about them was the *flow of consciousness* speech directed at me whenever we were together.

They talked about everything that came to their hearts and minds. The topics routinely turned from food to animals to TV shows to death and on and on. It was cute, special, and precious. They just always assumed that I wanted to hear what was on their minds—that I would listen and that I would care.

There is certainly a great need to have a regular time of prayer (during that daily time with God, our speaking to him *is* prayer), but that passage about praying without ceasing is more like that talk of my small children to me as *their* father.

Their openness in sharing with me so openly did not upset me; it was precious. I look back on it with great fondness. At night sometimes, they would fall asleep talking to me in the middle of a sentence. How precious! Their last words of the day were with me ...

Think about it. Rather than just thinking of prayer as some time kneeling on the floor with our heads bowed and eyes closed, what if we add to that a continual conversation throughout our day as we do what we do?

It's not that we're just blabbing about everything but that as we walk through the day, we learn to be in an ongoing conversation with the Father who loves us, our Abba-daddy.

I used to (when I was younger and had a lot more testosterone) be a bit shocked at the way an attractive woman could snag my attention, and I would start worrying, *What would God think about me looking at her like that?*

But then that is ridiculous. He knows what I'm looking at, he knows what I'm thinking, and he knows better than I do the why. Why would I try to impress my Daddy who made me when I am thinking something fleshly? Why not just bring it up and ask for some help in understanding and conquering my animalistic side?

Why not make those kinds of embarrassing moments part of our praying without ceasing?

So now, whatever the sinful thought, I try to just name it and say, "Wow, Abba, I'm not sure where I am, but help me with that!"

In the same vein, I spend a lot of time just expressing my joy and happiness when I see what he is doing in my life. Expressing my joy and gratitude for his hand in my life helps me to continually abide in him. It connects pleasure, laughter, and joy to the giver of those blessings.

Work on that continual conversation with God that constitutes "without ceasing."

4. *Love and hang—with the children.*

I've heard a number of parents state the principle of "if you want to show love to me, love my kids."

Where do you think that idea came from?

One of the most powerful and tangible ways to experience abiding in Christ is to choose to spend time with his other children.

In counseling people going through various struggles (addictions, loneliness, suicidality, marriage issues, etc.), I find that many if not most of those struggling lack close brothers and sisters in Christ. I know, we talked all about this in section I, but just wanted to hit it again.

There are no Lone Rangers in the family of Christ.

Seek out a few close brothers and sisters who can encourage you, and you them. Know that you need fellow believers you know well enough to share *anything* with, no matter how unflattering.

And they need you.

Do it.

5. *Mind your bathwater.*

I don't have a clue how many times I've brought this up already, but we are *bathed* in a strong fleshly culture. We have a veritable sewer pipe that we carry with us and sleep next to—the ubiquitous smartphone.

We have streaming television, twenty-four-hour "news" (propaganda), games that steal the precious hours of our lives, and food that bottoms out our energy and depletes our joy.

We choose this harm to ourselves.

Stop bathing in the sewer. Do not let your children bathe in poop.

The internet, smartphones, tablets, and television all have a function in the world, but these devices and the internet need to be dethroned from our lives.

Only God is worthy of sitting on the thrones of our lives.

It has been said that we become what we think about.

Choose what you think about. Make the choice to do what is pure, righteous, and brings a holy joy. Choose that which builds us up in the mind, body, and soul.

Go back to the chapter on un-hacking your life and use the guide in the appendix. Purify your life and the information that comes into your mind.

Summary

Those unchurched people all around us who lack peace, who have free-floating anxiety, they need to see the peace of Christ emanating from us. God's household should be remarkable in such a time of anxiety. If you or your little church family isn't, then what do we have to offer?

The lasting path to peace, fearlessness, friends, purpose,

love, and joy is found in abiding in Christ. All other choices are counterfeit, offering only a temporary reprieve from the angst of our age. Abiding is a deliberate choice. It is a hard habit to start, but the fruit of it is amazing.

If you are not experiencing peace in Christ, that is because you are choosing to not dwell in him. Back to the unimpressive Baptist pastor I referred to earlier—if we are not close, that's because we do not really want to be.

Let us draw near. Let us abide. We will not experience shalom simply because we get psyched up by a dynamic lesson from a pastor or by the rock concert music. Shalom comes from the Christ, from the Holy Spirit, and from the truth of God's holy Word.

May we, the "our, not my" family of God, show the world an accessible, free-floating *shalom!*

Dave out …

CHAPTER 13

The Ultimate Superpower

The world does not understand theology or dogma,
but it understands love and sympathy.
—Dwight L. Moody

To love someone means to see him as God intended him.
—Fyodor Dostoevsky

The chains of love are stronger than the chains of fear.
—William Gurnall

So now faith, hope, and love abide, these three;
but the greatest of these is love.
—Paul the apostle

~~~~~~~~~~~~~~~~~~~~~~~~~~~~~~~~~~~~~~

"I don't need someone to tell me what love is."

These were the words of a young husband who while traveling had met a young and beguiling divorcee and was now cheating on his wife.

Once he had confessed his affair to his covenant partner, she called me, and I tried to set up a meeting with him to talk him through this issue. His wife was willing to forgive and move on, but all this guy knew was that he was experiencing these intense feelings of attraction, pleasure, and acceptance in the arms of his lover.

His confusion is common in our times. Our media continually

portrays people *falling in love*, a mystical process that involves some intense feelings, an inability to think or speak, and obsessive thoughts. Great sex is usually a part of this Hollywood formula as well.

This guy was experiencing all of those—elements that are not love but involve some useful brain chemicals that our Creator gave us to help us toward and in our marriage relationships. If we believe that these elements constitute love, we are deluded.

This young hubby blew up his marriage for momentary chemical infatuation—not love. Love is a big problem for a lot of people—because of the way we were made.

We were made to be loved and to love.

Continuing with the theme of the book in being superheroes, the most impressive superpower we as the "our, not my" church demonstrate should be true love. There is a problem though. We too often do not show any significant difference from the world in this regard. Christian marriages should be so remarkable that a divorce between believers should make the local news.

Unfortunately, the divorce rate among believers is not substantially better than that of nonbelievers.

You know, we as God's children are immersed in a strong culture that continually portrays an image and concept of love that is counterfeit and unworkable. Not only that; the church is full of entertainment consumers. We no longer spend significant time in the Word, studying God's love, or time contemplating how that should play out in our marriages, families, churches, and with our neighbors.

When the lost encounter God's family, while they hear us speak of love, joy, and peace, they see right through us. We are just as anxious, depressed, sleep deprived, medicated, suicidal, morbidly obese, and confused as they are.

We, perhaps, are more polite in our mannerisms. We spend some time in a building singing and speak a language that could be called "Christianese."

We, as the "our, not my" family of God, need to gain wisdom on what the love that matters *is*. We need a working definition that we can spit out clearly and succinctly—so that we can walk in love.

Angry World

For my neighbors, friends, and even brothers and sisters in Christ who are under the sway of the mass delusion, I don't blame them for feeling anger.

Having no friends to draw close to in the struggles of life, feeling like you have no power or meaning, and being full of an anxiousness that you just can't seem to identify the source of—I perceive it would bring the anger out of any of us.

Further, experiencing an ongoing string of relationship failures as people use others for good feelings like a drug addict goes from hit to hit would tend to bring one to anger as well.

So we see a lot of angry outbursts around us, as well as angry-looking people.

What do the "our, not my" church have to offer angry people? Let us make sure *we* have this right before we dare think we have anything to offer the world.

Hey, You. What Is Love?

Yes, I'm talking to you.

As a teen, looking back, I'm pretty sure I was on the spectrum of autism. I even (as a young man) realized that I had a problem relating to people, and I did not like it. But in those days, we did not engage in the process of categorizing and limiting people by their disorders—and for that, I am thankful.

One of the good things about knowing I was different and realizing that I needed to change if I wanted to have healthy relationships is that I listened to and thought through the teachings I was hearing from a young preacher who came to our church.

He started by teaching us that love was not a feeling; rather, the choosing to do what is best in the interest of another. He pointed out that this was what Jesus demonstrated in coming to earth as man, showing us how to live in a difficult time, and dying for us.

I thought this through for years and even added to it. I ended up with, a few years into my marriage, the following definition of love that I had to go to at times when my attitude (or that of my wife) was not what it should be. I also had to go to it daily in my job and with my family.

I can honestly say that it made my marriage great. This definition of love provided me with strong and lasting friendships. This concept of love empowered me to walk into terrifying situations and share my faith.

The love of God is truly a superpower, and it will transform our church families and the world's perception of it if we can hold this clearly in our hearts and minds.

What is that definition that you should hold in your heart and mind?

I thought you'd never ask ...

By This We Know Love

The path by which I more thoroughly fleshed out the definition of love provided by the young preacher I mentioned took some time. I saw that the apostle John stated,

> By this we know love, that he (Jesus) laid down his life for us, and we ought to lay down our lives for the brothers. But if anyone has the world's goods and sees his brother in need, yet closes his heart against him, how does God's love abide in him?

Little children, let us not love in word or talk but in deed and in truth.[151]

John points out that in Jesus *laying down his life,* therein is found *love.* This is the agape form of love—often referred to properly as *the love of God.*

In thinking through what John was saying, it occurred to me that Yeshua the Messiah not only laid down his life at the cross but by being born. His proper place was at the right hand of God, in the most beautiful place out of this world—heaven.

He laid that down because *we needed it.*

He came down to do something for us *that would be the best thing for us.*

But look at his apparent mental state as he faces what is to be the greatest act of love in the history of humanity:

> Then Jesus went with them to a place called Gethsemane, and he said to his disciples, "Sit here, while I go over there and pray." And taking with him Peter and the two sons of Zebedee, he began to be sorrowful and troubled. Then he said to them, "My soul is very sorrowful, even to death; remain here, and watch with me." And going a little farther he fell on his face and prayed, saying, "My Father, if it be possible, let this cup pass from me; nevertheless, not as I will, but as you will."[152]

Notice what is missing. In this process of showing love to us, Jesus is not filled with giddy anticipation, breathless excitement, or obsessive feelings of how great we are.

He is, instead, filled with great sorrow, almost to the point of perceiving he could die from the stress of it. He is not about to do something because he feels internally good about it but because it is what we need the most.

He is also not doing it because we have been so good to him. He is doing it for the people who have been trying to stone and kill him. He is doing it for those who call him a fraud. He is doing it for the people who were on the way to take him to be beaten and crucified.

In other words, he is not loving us because we are responding appreciatively to his overtures.

From this amazing moment in the garden and beyond, we see the definition of love: *love is choosing to do what is in the best interest of another in spite of the way you feel or the way they respond.*

Memorize this definition. I'm serious. It is what I call *essential love*—because it not only provides what everyone around you needs, but it enables you to walk in love increasingly like our Savior did. It is essential that you be able to say this to yourself because it is vital that you be able to *do it.* I've carried this around for a few decades now. It is powerful because it is nothing more than, as John the apostle says, how we *know what love is.*

When things are tough and your attitude toward those around you is not what it should be, this definition can save you a lot of heartache. This kind of love requires faith to act upon, a confident knowledge that the Spirit of God dwells in you and that however you treat another person, you are taking the Spirit of God into that relationship and into that action.

This love becomes more natural and doable the closer you are in your walk with God. In effect, if someone asks you, "How is your prayer life?" and it seems hard to answer because you are conversing with him (and he with you) throughout the day, this type of close walking makes essential love doable. In your ongoing conversation throughout the day, if your mood deteriorates and you find yourself angry, feeling neglected, or hurt and you find yourself wanting to withhold love, that conversation that never ends (prayer without ceasing) makes it unlikely that you will sin by failing to love.

Once you have mastered that definition and begun to walk by it, there is another definition that I recommend you commit to your heart. This is what I call *nourishing love.* This is very similar to essential love, but it has a specific impact of building the quality of relationships and helps you to think less of yourself and more of others: *nourishing love is seeking to understand what speaks love to another person and then choosing to pursue opportunities to do those things.*

This obviously has power in any relationship, but the power within our church families and communities is huge. Being around people who act on this type of love resonates deeply within the heart of anyone who is isolated, lonely, and feeling meaningless. To be treated by others as significant, loveable, and accepted because of the intrinsic value that exists within each of us as image bearers of God—it calls deeply within us that this place, the place where we experience such love, is where we belong.

But How?

You may have a hard time envisioning how this happens in a traditional church setting. I do too.

My home church family was at around 1,100 members prior to the COVID nonsense—maybe about 650 now. Even at 650, it is very likely that people can come and visit for several services, largely unnoticed, and never return. Our eldership has long recognized that we need to *get small,* and we are moving that direction—but perhaps I can share how I handle it (and recommend others at my church do as well).

I do strongly believe in a living and active God—one who is placing me and others on a collision course of sorts, which places upon me the burden of what I have come to call "the stewardship of what God puts in front of me."

From the story of the Ethiopian Eunuch in Acts 8, verse 26 and following, we see that the Lord is aware of a man who needs, well, the Lord. His was a servant of the queen of the Ethiopians, and he was returning from Jerusalem, where he had been worshipping the Hebrew God. An angel sends Philip the apostle to where this man's chariot will be passing and has him "join" (i.e., run alongside of) the chariot and strike up a conversation.

Think about the size of the world, the number of unique individuals in it, and that God is aware of where each one is and what they need. It is stunning. He cares for this servant of the queen, and he places someone in his life (beside his chariot, running!) to lead him to where he needs to be.

I serve *that* God. So do you.

It's hard for me to describe, but I perceive that our Lord routinely shows me someone in my church, or anywhere else I go, that I am to "join." The number of times I have seen this *joining* result in some amazing spiritual growth and glory to God is astounding. And just to be clear, often God joins someone with me who helps me to grow!

I'm not all that! I need encouragement, love, and challenge just like anyone else. I am not God's gift to the world. I'm just a beloved but weak child of the King of the universe.

Further, as someone who does a bit of part-time therapy work (I call it peer-counseling), I realized at one point that I had never helped anyone who didn't also help me. Their challenges, their sorrows, and their solutions—plus their friendship—spurred me on to greater love for God.

I encourage you to, in view of the truth that our God knows us all (the lost, the saved, and the seeking), *walk with expectancy* that God is working around and through you, every moment of every day.

While the somewhat traditional church services that my family of God engages in do not give any substantial opportunity to reach out, the times before and after certainly do. Small groups, discipling, and smaller classes can be a great opportunity too.

The Challenges of Loving

Our world is very messed up.
It always has been.

Many of us (if not most) fall into the category of people the apostle Paul spoke of:

> Do not be deceived: neither the sexually immoral, nor idolaters, nor adulterers, nor men who practice homosexuality, nor thieves, nor the greedy, nor drunkards, nor revilers, nor swindlers will inherit the kingdom of God. *And such were some of you.*[153]

When it comes to loving messed-up people, there is likely a fear of someone taking advantage of us, of using us, of just pretending to be interested in spiritual things because they need something.

There is a concurrent fear that if we reach out to a messed-up and hurting person, we will not have the resources to deal with their issues.

Both are legitimate concerns.

The challenging thing about that "such were some of you" passage above is that Paul said that in dealing with the very issue of someone who is a brother or sister treating someone wrongly! He was strongly condemning people in the brotherhood for their "going to law" against each other and instead commends this approach: "Why not rather suffer wrong? Why not rather be defrauded?"[154]

Truly loving someone, or attempting to, carries a risk. That hurts.

Jesus knows it better than any of us, right?

The desire to control the response of others, to limit our risk, to prevent ourselves from suffering—it isn't Christlike. Jesus showed great love to the disciples he took on, knowing prophetically that one of them would sell him out. In a way, all of them would. Back to what we discussed earlier. When we come to Christ, we are called to die to self, so when someone betrays our love, we are simply experiencing what our Lord and brother experienced on a much larger scale.

Cold Ministry

Another issue facing us as the folks who assault the gates of hell is that, as an army, we do not train for battle.

My church family for years has done a community outreach dinner around Thanksgiving. We invite folks who are struggling financially, and our church comes together to cook a great dinner, provide coats, and even give them food to take home.

One year, I wasn't going to be able to participate because of work, so I didn't sign up. But then my schedule changed, so I went—and had nothing to do. So as the guests started arriving in our big area where we eat, I just went out and talked with people.

It was an eye-opener.

Here were all these people we were supposed to be blessing, hoping perhaps that they would join our church family.

I was sitting out with the visitors or kneeling beside their chairs and chatting.

Lined up along the walls of the room were the church members who came to serve food, but the food wasn't ready yet. They had their backs against the wall, some talking to one another. Most of our guests sat at the tables, some talking among themselves if they had a friend or family member with them. Some were sitting in silence.

Us.

Them.

That was what I perceived the mood of the night was.

Understand, I love my church family dearly. They are amazingly loving people. So why did they seem so aloof and unloving on this night?

It's a common problem, becoming more normal every day.

While our small children learn to make sound and converse with their mouths pretty early on, it is rare that anyone trains us to start and sustain conversations with people we do not know.

The good news is this skill can be learned, and it is way easier than you might think.

As I mentioned earlier, I was a bit on the autism spectrum growing up. Talking with people was exceedingly difficult for me. It made for a very lonely existence.

Over the years, I studied, practiced, and grew in my abilities to initiate and keep conversations going with just about anybody. My wife sometimes calls me "talk-a-matic"; it's hard to shut me up now. We'll cover some more of the ways we as the "our, not my" church can prepare ourselves to lovingly communicate in the next section, but simply learning to talk is an essential component of our armament as the gates of hell assaulting army that we are. It has been said that *communication is the highway on which love travels.*

People need to connect with others in talk, so talking to the needy is as important, or likely more important, than feeding or giving money.

Love Trumps Anger

The big point about the ultimate superpower of the love of God is that it is the perfect antidote to the generalized sense of anger that has infected our society under the influence of mass delusion. The body of Christ needs to be a place where people feel truly loved. Interestingly, that does not mean that we accept everything as being okay.

We follow what Yeshua modeled as one who ate with tax collectors, prostitutes, and sinners—that he accepted all as image bearers of God and precious in the sight of the Father. At the same time, when someone is engaged in sin, that sin is destructive to the person and others, so we do what is best for them ultimately. We let them gently know when the trust is there that they need to work with God to stop the sinning.

God's commands are not arbitrary, nor are they indicators of old cultural norms brought forward. They are eternal truths.

The challenge for any church, though, is that in order to speak into the lives of someone engaged in rebellion against God, we will have far more influence if there is a relationship of love and trust first.

We accept people as image bearers of God who are sinning. We work to bring them to holiness as they are able to accept it.

I had one middle-aged man in my class who had been through alcohol and drug rehab. He had experienced some amazing victories through a faith-based recovery program. Our class for a few weeks focused on holy sexuality, and after the second class, he came up to me in tears with his live-in girlfriend. "I never thought of giving *that* part of my life over to God!"

He was ashamed and disappointed in himself.

I asked him, "So do you think you could have quit drugs, alcohol, and wrongful sex all at the same time?"

He shook his head no, still crying.

"God is patient. He knows you can only handle so much at one time. Maybe he wants you to focus on this issue now," I said.

He gave me a big hug.

He went on and married the woman and has a beautiful family, as God intended. His sharing with me was based on a relationship of trust. He knew that I had many struggles when I was younger and still had some to that day. We stood before God together as sinners in need of a Savior.

Love in action.

Church, let's do this ...

Dave out ...

SECTION III

The Practical Superhero Doing What God Puts in Front of You

CHAPTER 14

Learn to Use Your Mouth

Who has made man's mouth? Who makes him
mute, or deaf, or seeing, or blind?
Is it not I, the LORD?
—The LORD Almighty

It is greed to do all the talking but not to want to listen at all.
—Democritus

It was impossible to get a conversation going, everybody was talking too much.
—Yogi Berra

~~~~~~

The resting kill face.

Most of us have probably heard about it. Do you own one?

I have a dear friend, but we almost didn't become friends. He had some trouble in his marriage, and so he came to me—the church marriage guy. I had never felt very drawn to approach him, but I didn't mention it until years later as to why.

We were talking, several years after our friendship had deepened, after he had moved away to be closer to family. He was talking about my (and formerly our) church family and made the statement, "When we first got there, it was very cliquish. It was not very friendly."

It was time for me to be loving in an honest but difficult way.

"You know, I gotta be honest with you. Do you realize how you look when you are sitting in church or anywhere else? You look like you are about to hurt somebody! Your face and posture say, 'Leave me alone!'"

It was true. He and his wife are wonderful, loving people. But their resting posture and facial expressions are not welcoming.

The truth is a lot of us are that way. So many of us are insecure, afraid that others will reject us, yet desiring deep down that people will love us as we are.

But we are at the same time afraid of being discovered.

So let's start this chapter on learning to initiate and sustain conversations with the following principle:

1. *Most people may appear to not want to talk. Don't buy it.*

Practically, if God draws your attention to someone, but they seem to not be approachable, just say, "They're insecure and a bit scared, just like me." And then move toward them.

One of my best female friends is a good example of this. She always looked so secure, content, and not reaching out for contact. She was always well dressed, hair and makeup were impeccable, and she was obviously accomplished and intelligent.

Yet my Lord kept putting her in front of me, so I started talking to her, and as we shall see, I mainly asked questions and listened with my heart.

A couple of years later, she had helped me with a project, and I thanked her for all she had done. What she said next was very telling: "Thank you for talking to me."

Wow. In spite of what she appeared to be, she had the same need to connect—and apparently, she often felt isolated. She, like I had been, was a bit on the introverted side but wanted to change. She appeared to be okay not talking, but she needed someone to engage her.

The big lesson here is *if the Spirit of God leads you to someone, initiate a friendship. Talk with them.*

Moving onward, the next big problem (or so it seems) is exactly how do we initiate conversation with someone who we do not know and who appears not to want to talk? Here is the next principle of initiating and sustaining conversations:

2. *To get words flowing, use a nonthreatening initiator.*

This has been one of the biggest ah-ha moments for me that has enabled me to talk with people from every background. An *initiator* is simply a safe way to get someone to talk, usually about themselves but sometimes about a situation that you are both in. Here are a few verbal initiators:

- *The "thingy."* This is the one that I most frequently use. A *thingy* is something the person is wearing (jewelry, medallion, hair style, tattoo, or ?) that you can say something about, often in the form of a question.

As an example, I love ornately braided hair. So when I am drawn to someone with such a hairstyle, I'll just say, "Wow, I love your hair! How long did it take to get that done?" I've had a lot of good conversations starting with a little talk of braiding, how long it lasts, and my lack of hair.

If you notice a unique piece of jewelry, a T-shirt with a college or sporting team, or even a computer with a brand name on it, all are good ways to get a conversation going.

I had a guy in Clive, Iowa, use this tactic on me. My wife had given me one of the very thin MacBook Air computers when it was a fairly new product. I was using it in a coffee shop when a man stepped up to my table and asked, "How do you like your Air?"

It was hilarious. For a moment, I thought, *How do I like my air? Through my nose, 78 percent nitrogen, 21 percent oxygen, 1 percent trace gases,*" until I realized he was asking about my computer. Our conversation went from computers to a discussion of emotional intelligence and the failure of the public education system (i.e., government schooling) to prepare our young people for life.

The *thingy* is a great tool for starting a conversation leading to a friendship.

You can use tattoos ("Whoa, tell me about that one), clothing ("That dress is stunning. Where did you get it?"), cars ("How do you like your EV?"), organizational pins or medallions ("I like your cross. Are you Christian?"), or just about anything else different about a person that isn't embarrassing.

- *Feel with.* It's interesting. I've been called out for claiming "I'm good" when I wasn't. One really good friend sat down in front of me, after he had asked how I was doing, and said, "Steve, I see something on your face that isn't good. What's going on with you, buddy?"

He was right. I love being the guy with the answer, and I so appreciated being called out for trying to be the hero when I needed a hero.

He became my hero, by starting serious and somber where my heart really was.

Empathy means to *feel with.* We humans usually can, if we choose to, sense when someone is down, worried, or stressed.

If we choose, that can be a great way to start a conversation.

Not that we say, "You seem really down," but instead, we go to them and try to approach them in a similar mood.

If God is pointing you in someone's direction, and as you observe them, they seem distracted and worried, don't go bouncing up joyfully and say, "Hey! I love that dress! Where did you get it?"

No. When you perceive a quiet and pensive mood, come up beside them and quietly ask, "Hey, you seem a little sad. Are you okay?"

In our isolated society, too many people have no one to talk to or to share their pain. Just asking, "Are you okay?" can set you off on a multihour conversation and friendship if you have the time.

Conversely, if you see someone who is bursting with excitement,

"Whoa, you seem really up. What happened to you today?" can be another lead-in to connecting to another lonely person who needs a friend—and who needs our Savior.

3. *Talk about normal and boring stuff.*

Small talk is underrated. Talking about ordinary and even the boring aspects of life is a great way to break the ice. With my airline job, I've spent hundreds of hours packed in the back of an airline in coach. Of course, you can start with a *thingy* and match the mood—but what next?

In coach class, I'm often in a seat section with three people, and our bags are stuffed under the seats in front of us. I have long legs, so I'll say, "I need to learn to pack lighter. You know, it's kind of tight in these seats!" It is a boring and nonoriginal way I get people talking. It breaks the ice. Nearly everyone tries to bring too much stuff with them when they travel. The ordinary conversation can lead to the extraordinary.

"What do you do when you're not here?" is another boring topic. I use this or a form of this everywhere I go. If I'm getting my haircut, for instance, and I don't know the person doing the work, I'll ask, "What do you like to do when you're not cutting hair?"

The main point here is just to help people loosen up so you can begin to form a friendship—and hopefully go deeper.

The interesting thing about the isolation so prevalent in our society today is that most people will move past the ordinary and boring topics quickly; all you have to do is listen carefully for an opener (they reveal something that is bothering them or that motivates them) and then up the quality of your questions.

"So how's life going for you these days?" is surprisingly effective. I've asked that several times and still had the person bearing their soul twenty-five minutes later! It is not uncommon for people to reveal very personal details and then ask something like, "What do you think I should do?"

That is usually the point where I use the next principle.

4. Ask about their religious beliefs. I normally say something like "Do you have any religious background?" So far, I've never had anyone get angry or not answer this.

Yes, I know that *everyone* is religious. Religion at its core is just a way we make sense of the world.

If you ask this question, and someone gets a bit defensive or hostile, learn the following response:

- Stay calm and listen.
- If they are hostile, just apologetically say something like, "I'm sorry. I just like to hear what people believe about the nature of life. I'm not trying to pry."

In years of doing this, though, I've yet to have anyone get very upset. I had one guy who said, "I don't talk about religion or politics at work." So I talked about religion for the first hour, then politics the second. Actually, I asked a lot of questions that led him to talk about it! At the end of it (we were in the cockpit at 35,000 feet, flying to the West Coast), he said, "You know, that was really refreshing to talk about those things!" He is still a good friend.

The thing to remember leads us to this next point. Be in listening mode, not "win the argument and convert them to Christ in one conversation" mode.

5. Friend, not project. Clear your heart of the idea of "we need to build up our church attendance." Instead, follow the model of Joshua of Nazareth, the guy we call Jesus. He was somewhat scandalous in that he ate with the "tax collectors and sinners."[155] I get the impression that our Savior, while on earth, was great to hang around with.

As we've noted, the isolated people of today could use someone like that in their life! Start with a friendship. Listen to the Spirit. If you perceive that maybe there is an opportunity to go deep into a spiritual issue with someone you've just met, go there! Perhaps someone else has already laid the groundwork with this precious person.

But do not go in seeing this *person* as a *project.*

People need connection, acceptance, and love—not just attention for what they would see as "your" benefit. Sure, we can spiritualize the making a person a project by claiming, "I'm just worried about their spiritual status." But really, unless God has already been doing some serious work in their lives (and often he has; that is the next principle), you need to develop some trust before you can speak into their hearts.

Be a friend, be a good listener, and allow the Lord to add them to his church through whatever means he chooses.

6. *Planting or watering?* I was once asked by a preacher friend of mine to speak at a youth event with the topic "Does the Church Need to Change?"

In my faith tradition, this can be a difficult topic, one fraught with emotion. We assume (as do most groups?) that we are doing things right.

But I went about it in a different way. I just really looked at my church family and asked the question, "What really needs to change?"

My answer, and thus my topic, was *I need to change.*

As I prepared for this topic (I had about six weeks), I saw that as a member of the "our, not my" called-out ones, I routinely failed to be a good steward of the people God put in front of me at work. In preparation for this talk, I vowed to God that I would talk with every man or woman I flew with for the next six weeks and see precisely where they were spiritually.

It was amazing. Although I was nervous and anticipating some pushback, offense, and maybe even getting turned in for being *too evangelistic* (this had happened to at least one pilot where I worked), instead I found that every single person I worked with in that six weeks was in the middle of a significant spiritual struggle.

This illustrates the truth that our God knows all people, and he orchestrates people with spiritual needs to cross paths with his children who can help provide that need through the leading and words provided by the Holy Spirit.

One guy I talked to had been having intense discussions with his wife about "returning to their faith." They had stopped being part of a church early in their marriage, but now that their children were getting older, they were realizing that something important was missing in their family's life.

Another man was struggling in his concern for an adult daughter who had gotten into a religious group with some (to him) strange-sounding beliefs that he did not know how to answer biblically.

Be alert to these kinds of opportunities where God has been working and you can step into more than just a friendship role more quickly. It truly is amazing and faith building when you see that our Lord *does* orchestrate our daily lives.

7. *Advanced training—get it!* So I did this *thing*. I bought a book, I did the mp3 download version, and even purchased a bigger advanced course. One day after church, it happened. I was given an opportunity to apply all that I had studied, learned, and mentally prepared for.

While I was talking with friends after church, a good friend of mine walked over with a guy in tow. This guy was early twenties, deathly pale, and wearing black. He had a very troubled look on his face.

My friend said, "Hey, this guy needs to talk to someone, and I knew you were good at that sort of thing."

I introduced myself and suggested we find a quieter place to sit and talk. We went into my classroom and sat down. I asked how I could help.

"I need to talk to someone about some demons I'm struggling with," he said flatly.

"Okay, so just so you know, I'm a believer in Jesus Christ, and I offer advice from that standpoint. Is that okay?"

"Yes, I just really need to talk," he stated.

"So do you have any religious beliefs of your own?" I queried.

"Have you ever heard of *Thelema*?" he asked.

Now this is the point that I used to worry about—and I perceive it stops a lot of us from talking with strangers about matters of faith.

I had never heard of *Thelema*, so in the past, I would have been scared or nervous. How do you talk to someone out of a belief in something you have no clue about? But because of *that book* and *that training* I had, I was calm. I just applied what I had been trained to do.

In my genuinely interested tone, I said, "No. What is Thelema?"

He got a bit more animated. He explained that it was an amalgamation of beliefs. The founder, Alister Crowley, had looked through all of the world's greatest religions and taken their best teachings and synthesized them together into a philosophy of life that he (the pale guy I was talking to) really appreciated and found helpful.

"That sounds like a great idea!" I replied. "So could you sum it up for me as to what difference it makes in your life?"

"Crowley summed it up as, 'Do as thou wilt.'" He seemed happy with this concise summary of his current philosophy of life.

I had another question. It was what *that* training taught me to do. It also, I perceive, was a question straight from the Holy Spirit, because the Lord was working on this guy. "So, 'Do as thou wilt.' Hmm, so if there's a fifty-year-old guy who 'wilts' (wants to) have sex with an eight-year-old little boy, then that's okay according to Thelema?"

"No, no, that's not what I'm saying. That would hurt ..."

"I'm with you on that. In my Christian faith, it is wrong—because every person is created in the image of God and is to be protected and loved, but if it's just about doing what *you* think is right, and you think it is right to go after a little boy, then who's to say you're wrong?" I pointed out.

"But you can't, umm, it's not right to, oh, this makes so much more sense when I'm not talking to you!" he said.

Notice what happened and what *that* training enabled me to do.

I knew nothing about his belief system other than what he told me. I did know the *truth* of scripture, and I had *that* training, which taught me to listen carefully, apply what I heard to its logical conclusion, and ask a question that allowed the person with the false belief to *take apart their own argument!*

Do you want to be able to take apart any argument without understanding it from the beginning? Do you want to stay in control of an argument such as this one and reach to the core of a badly thought-out heresy?

If so, then the book I read is called *Tactics: A Game Plan for Discussing Your Christian Convictions* by Gregory Koukl.[156] His training is so effective, so complete, and so accessible that all I can do is recommend that you buy the book *and* go to www.str.org and sign up for STR University. The university is an online course that will equip you to do just what I did with a guy I didn't know believing in something I had never heard of.

Tactics, as Greg Koukl points out, puts you in the driver's seat of conversations. It allows you to be a true listener and treat the person you are talking to with dignity.

Summary

We learn to talk by listening to those we are around as small children, but how many of us have really been trained to listen well, think well about what we hear, and ask good questions?

Further, how many of us have even learned how to initiate conversations and sustain them?

We, as God's called out, must take being equipped to speak seriously if we are to be who God intended us to be. As he puts us in the path of people who need him, will the opportunity find us ready and able?

I pray that you (and your little group of "our, not my" family) will learn to connect and make a difference in the lives of the lost and struggling!

Dave out ...

CHAPTER 15

Being Who God Says You Are Where He Places You

Blessed is the influence of one true, loving human soul on another.
—George Eliot

Grace is the beauty of form under the influence of freedom.
—Friedrich Shiller

You don't have to be a 'person of influence' to be influential.
In fact, the most influential people in my life are probably
not aware of the things they've taught me.
—Scott Adams

We are ambassadors for Christ, God making his appeal through us.
—Paul the apostle

Let your light shine before others, so that they may see your good
works and give glory to your Father who is in heaven.
—Yeshua of Nazareth, the Messiah

T hey didn't like me much.

When I finished my training as a military pilot and got back to my home unit, I figured out pretty quickly that this was the wrong place for a believer in Jesus Christ to be. These guys were hard-drinking, womanizing, profane, and somewhat abusive people.

I got yelled at and threatened a few times for being a "holier-than-thou" Christian. Once was because I refused to go to a strip club for my initiation as a newbie copilot. I also chose not to go out drinking, and I differed with my comrades over the idea that what happened on a trip stayed on the trip (i.e., when a married guy took a girl to his room on a military mission, it was understood to be secret). I believed that anything I did anywhere could be shared with my wife or anyone else.

I became very disliked very quickly.

I actually looked into going to law school or even learning to shoe horses in order to be in a more Christian-friendly environment (I know, law school? What was I thinking?). After all the hard work of earning my wings, I was contemplating giving it up to be in a more morally tame environment.

Eleven years later, I was leading a Sunday-morning worship service with a bunch of guys from my unit while deployed on a mission. I was just starting to share a message from the Word when my eyes met with those of one of the guys in my unit—who about ten years earlier had cornered me and shouted at me in front of everyone. He had told me that I was a worthless scumbag and shouldn't be in this unit.

He was now my commander and was sitting across from me with his Bible open in his lap.

"This is weird," I stated.

He laughed and said, "You preach, brother. You preach."

It was hard, and it was joyous. It was hard because I thought of my lack of faith in thinking that I should have left this group of people because they were so ungodly. It was hard because this guy, this abuser—well, I had written him off as irredeemable.

The irredeemable was now my brother?

What a joy!

You see, what my Abba has taught me and countless others is that his mission of reconciliation works best when his people choose to be faithful where he puts them. I had wanted to be a military pilot since at least the time I was twelve. Where did that desire come from?

I now suspect it was something my Father put within me—to show his surpassing glory and overwhelming love to these ungodly reprobates, myself included in that same group.

Sure, they behaved badly. But *I doubted* the good news of Jesus Christ would ever reach their hearts. Which status of reprobate was worse?

He not only reached them; he turned them into vibrant and bold believers who put me to shame in their enthusiastic evangelizing.

He used me and a small group of believers in my unit and elsewhere, along with a few select life crises, to break through the hard hearts of some hard-partying and self-centered men. He also transformed my doubting heart and weak faith.

My fellow believers (they seemed to be few and far between at first) felt incapable and weak—and that was true. We couldn't change these men in our own strength.

But our Abba didn't expect us to. He just needed us to be where he had put us, to love, to endure a little abuse, and to be a halfway decent example of our Savior. The people he sent us to needed examples of followers who had a Savior because they *needed* a Savior. The Lord God Almighty would do the all heavy lifting—and did he ever!

That's the way the mission works.

Points of Light—A Different Vision

Sometime after that, I started a small ministry. It didn't go very far, because my Father taught me yet another lesson I and likely you need to know.

I was endeavoring to get more believers to be aware of the important political issues going on and get involved in calling their various representatives—whether local, state, or national.

This idea started small. I just printed out a small newsletter and handed it to people and encouraged them to take at least an hour a week to call, write, or do something to make sure that righteous voices were being heard on the important moral issues.

But as I pondered how to make this ministry more effective, I realized that I needed to reach more people. I had this vision of America being in darkness, and little outposts of my ministry needed to be planted all over the land, where those involved would spread this light of righteousness in our political dealings.

That was the end of my musings—for I recognized that this *structure* was nothing new. I was the *church of the Christ!*

The problem is we have the points, but very little light emanates from them. The church far too often is dark. This cannot be allowed to continue. As John the apostle notes, "In him [Jesus] is no darkness at all."[157]

Perhaps one of the biggest challenges to God's people in making an impact on our society today is found in the *ministry* concept itself. We see ministry and missions as something we *go do.* We get on an airliner and fly to a distant place, work there for a week or two, and we have done mission work. Or we join a ministry at church, and we consider our ministry/mission box checked.

And certainly, we have likely done something good.

But think about what would happen if we embraced the reality of what I experienced in my military unit every day and in every way.

What if every stay-at-home mother viewed her time with her children, husband, and in her neighborhood as her mission and ministry? What if she embraced that her place in the world for that phase of life was a sacred calling? What if she saw each of her neighbors, no matter how scary or annoying, as a God-given stewardship? In effect, what if God placed her with her husband, her children, and in that neighborhood, and in that house, condo, or apartment for the reason of glorifying himself? What if she had the attitude that God placed her little family right in that spot in the world because there were people who needed to be reached and love to be given? What if she embraced that those living in darkness around her needed her little family to be the light?

Vocation Writ Large

The big picture is what I saw when I was trying my little ministry—we are in a country that is experiencing *increasing* darkness. If instead of "going" (or perhaps in addition to going) on short-term missions and doing some isolated task on occasion that we *call* ministry—if we woke up each morning expecting God to be placing opportunities to engage *his priorities in mission and ministry* to appear all around us—what an amazing difference it would make! It would, I contend, transform our society.

What if every believer in your "our, not my" called-out community woke up each day with a mission mentality, fully confident that whatever the day was like, they would see and experience the hand of God on their life. What if I *know* that even in the most mundane or unpleasant of days, I have purpose and possibility *that* day?

That term *vocation* at the header—it is derived from a word meaning *calling.* It is an old word from believers of past days reflecting this very truth that we are discussing. God gives you abilities, desires, and capabilities, all of which work together to place you where he needs you for a purpose that is his.

Instead of "going to work" or "staying home with the kids and doing housework," what if we *fully embraced* our vocation from God. What if instead of waiting for our *moment of ministry* or contemplating changing our "career" to *go into the ministry,* what if we just accepted where our Lord has placed us today and the skills/title/responsibilities as having come from him?

Taking my personal experience of being in the military in a *bad environment for a Christian,* do you look into the political realm and wish that someone with integrity, courage, and a love for God would step up and seek office? What if that desire is from God himself, and you are the one he is *calling into the ministry?* Is that concern with *politics* (another old word that basically conveyed the meaning of "of the citizens," not a bad thing!) something that God placed in your heart because he needs you to step up? Instead of being someone seeking to be a politician who happens to be a believer, what if you become a politician because your Creator equipped you and placed you here for that purpose?

Sure, it looks like a horrible environment for a believer—something that perhaps you feel incapable of dealing with? You would be right, just like I was right in my early days in the military. I didn't have the power to correct and convert all of these people; that power resides in the God that I serve. I just had to be faithful to love God and the people he put in front of me each day.

By the time I left my unit, going to work was very much like going to church! In fact, given that "church" is the called out, and my unit had become a large group of dedicated believers, it was a de facto church!

Thus, if you have political interests and concerns given to you from God, along with a few hundred or thousand other believers, might not our ugly situation be transformed if we considered and accepted that calling?

In fact, the Bible account is full of people who were called to serve absolutely wicked governments. Lot had a place in the "gates" of Sodom. The gates in those days were the place of local government. Daniel served in more than one pagan regime. Deborah was called to become "awake" and lead Israel during a time when the men around her were cowering in fear.

In fact, Deborah is a great case study to demonstrate something that our God was very concerned about—and why it is vital we start to see our lives as an orchestrated calling to be on mission every day and in every way.

After Deborah led Israel to victory over their oppressor nation, she broke out in song. Her song is very instructive about her view of God, God's view of her society's situation, and her view of how she and her fellow community members needed to live. Here is the first, and perhaps the most important, point she shares with us:

> In the days of Shamgar, son of Anath, in the days of Jael, the highways were abandoned, and travelers kept to the byways. The villagers ceased in Israel; they ceased until I arose; I Deborah, arose as a mother in Israel.[158]

She paints a bleak picture of what life had come to be around her. People were afraid to travel the good roads. Some versions say "village life ceased" instead of villagers, but the meaning is clear either way.

The people in her community were isolated and fearful, and she saw it. God called her to step up to "mother" her people. In fact, in her song, there is a rebuke of people who *did not see* the pressing need of *mission and ministry* where they had been placed by God:

> Among the clans of Reuben, there were great searchings of heart. Why did you sit still among the sheepfolds, to hear the whistling for the flocks ... Gilead stayed beyond the Jordan; and Dan, why did he stay with the ships? Asher sat still.[159]

To unpack her critique, which I understand to be *God's critique,* God had placed men of strength in her community and nation *for the purpose of pursuing what mattered to him.* From Deborah's song, we see that one thing that really mattered to him was *village life* for the children he loved!

Looking at the pattern of our Creator's plan, after he created man, he created someone for him to commune *with.* We, being made in the image of God—who is the three-in-one relational Deity—are also created to live in community with others. When that community stopped (because the men of Deborah's time saw their purpose as living in fear to preserve their own skin? This is self-idolatry.), God did something very unusual in Israel. He called a woman and a mother to stand up and demand that the men of her day do their mission where he had placed them to do it!

While churches have been on the decline for several decades now, there are still millions of believers in America going to church each week. What would happen if we expanded our concept of *mission* and *ministry* to include serving wherever we are—at home, work, or in political office?

Once Deborah woke her communities up, she noted that God granted success and praised some folks for getting this very important truth about who God says we are and where he places us:

> That the leaders took the lead in Israel, that the people offered themselves willingly, bless the LORD ... Zebulun is a people who risked their lives to the death; Napthali, too, on the heights of the field.[160]

While Deborah lived in a time of physical warfare, let there be no missing the truth that she as well as *we* live in times of ongoing spiritual warfare. We must expand our vision of not only who we are but begin (if you are not there already) to be people who live boldly on mission in every aspect of life. Let's provide a few practical ideas in a few possible areas.

On Mission Where You Live

About that place you live—whether it is a starter home, a palatial crib, condo, or apartment—may I be so bold as to suggest that our Lord placed you there for reason. He put you in your neighborhood to be a shining light, an encourager, and an example of how filled with light life can be when you know *the Light*.

What is strange so often in American society today is that

although the houses (and obviously apartments and condos) are often very close together, our neighbors might as well live beyond visual range. As a society, we are very isolated, cocooned in our comfy little homes with the constant companionship of the blue light of smartphones, tablets, computers, and HDTVs.

The COVID lockdowns have seemingly made our isolation habits worse, even once they ended. There was a significant shift in working and doing school from home, further isolating people from others. While I have heard many say that they *prefer* this isolated work structure, the impact of digital interaction is starting to show; it isn't good.

Professor Mattia Desmet notes the following about digital shortcomings compared to in-person interactions:

> When people talk to each other, they sense each other very sharply because they perceive the slightest changes in intonation, voice timbre, facial expression, body position, rate of speech, and so on. Like flocking starlings, they form one organism. They are connected with one another through a psychic membrane that transfers the slightest ripple in the body and soul. In every exchange of words, no matter how trivial, people show themselves to be perfect dance partners; they are subtly united through the eternal music of language.[161]

Get it? Our Creator *designed* us to interact deeply through face-to-face communication. Even if people have retreated to their homes in fear, the fruit of that fear (as with most fears) is harmful to well-being.

As to the impact of digital interaction, Desmet importantly notes the following:

This complex phenomenon [the face-to-face interaction above] degrades when digitized. Digital interactions always have a certain delay; exclude certain aspects of contact, such as scent and temperature, are selective (you only see someone else's face); and create the constant, preapprehension that the connection may drop. As a result, digital interactions are not only experienced as reticent and stiff; they also give us the feeling that we cannot really (physically) sense the other. In the words of workplace leadership expert Gianpiero Petriglieri: "In digital interactions, our minds are tricked into believing that we are together, but our bodies know that we are not; what's so exhausting about digital conversations is being constantly in the presence of another's absence.[162]

Desmet's book, *The Psychology of Totalitarianism*,[163] is the newest book on my must-read list for believers in the Bible. It details how those with tyrannical desires exploit and corrupt our designed nature in order to instill fear and compliance. This book is vital to our understanding of why we need to be, as Christ followers, who we are wherever we are.

Being Who God Says You Are Where You Live

Let us consider a few ways in which our *home* can be an outpost of light:

1. Embrace the truth that you are living where you are living for God's purposes.

I have to give credit and make another of my top book recommendations for all believers. *The Gospel Comes with a House Key*[164] by Rosaria Butterfield opened my eyes more fully to the impact of living where God places you. I mentioned her work earlier. She shares the touching story of an interaction with a rather unusual neighbor and makes the point that pierced my heart a few years ago when I first read it. Up till then, I had made the application of being who God made me at work, but this challenged me on my front porch (and still does):

> "Why are we friends?" my awkward neighbor Hand asks as we are walking our dogs during a two o'clock, mid-afternoon homeschool break, on a mild, fall North Carolina day, the blue sky shouting its glory for all to behold. Hank, a little light-sensitive, twitches as his eyes adjust to the noon sun. He looks like he has just woken up.
>
> "I mean, why don't you think I'm an eyesore and an oddball, like my neighbors in Chatham did?"
>
> One of the many things I love about Hank: his bold questions, never holding back anything that others bury in social acceptance.
>
> *"Because God never gets the address wrong,"* I reply.

Her book offers some very practical ways to be faithful to the place where God placed you to live. For now, let's just say that we all need to accept this truth as Ms. Butterfield does.

2.   *Practice the talking skills we talked about. Get to know your neighbors.*

At one point in our current house, we had a young couple move in the house across the back fence. I decided, "I need to go start a friendship with them."

One day, I was working near the fence, and I saw the young lady walking toward the fence. We met (for the first time) and began that friendship.

I asked them how long they had been living there and was shocked. "Eight years" was the answer! I had sat on my obedience to be light in my neighborhood for *eight years.* Further, as I made conversation and asked that very same question I shared earlier about them having a religious background, she said, "You know, we've really wanted to start going to church. We were just a little nervous about going where no one knew us."

Wow. Just wow.

In other words, here was a young couple, now with kids, who would have happily welcomed someone to go with to get to know our God! They would have welcomed a conversation over the fence, around the grill, or in one of our homes about the Savior in whom there is hope and joy.

You never know such needs and desires if you do not know your neighbors.

A couple of years after that, that couple moved out, and a new couple moved in.

I saw them home within the first few days after they moved in. I walked through the snow with some banana bread and the first book I had written. The new lady had the door open to welcome me when I was still fifty feet away!

Why had I waited so long?

Fear.

But what I found out was that God was already working on my neighbors. All I really have to do is just extend the hand of friendship and a warm smile and have the courage to start a conversation.

So wherever you are, make a deliberate effort to just be a friend.

3. *Be a connector.*

As you get to know your neighbors, start inviting folks over to introduce them to the other neighbors. Have a little cookout or a pot of soup and just have a friendly "getting to know you" session. It's a good way just to be honest in your faith. It is likely that most people are facing some challenges. You can always ask before you bless the food if anyone has something you can pray for. You can ask them to pray for something going on in your life.

As you may already know more people than those neighbors who have been there longer than you, you can also tell them about the other people living nearby. We have found this to be helpful. My wife was able to tell of the passing of one of our neighbor's wife to someone we were visiting. They were unaware and deeply moved.

Think of the power of becoming someone who *loves* others around them—once again, not as a project but as someone who sees others as made in the image of God and thus worthy of being loved. How does that look to your neighbors? When they are hurting or in need, who might they go to? The isolated neighbor or the one who cares about and rallies help for others?

As you get to know people and have them over, this is a great way to introduce your isolated neighbors to one another. This is a way to build *village life* that we spoke of earlier from the story of the judge Deborah in the Old Testament.

4. *Make your house the place to go.*

I know this is kind of scary, but if over time you are consistently loving your neighbors and it comes to be known that you are the person who helps in times of need, then they also need to know *where to go* and *who to call* when they need help or information about other neighbors.

This can be inconvenient. It can cost you some money, but do you have the heart and warmth, and do you plan to have a bit of extra food and drink on hand? When someone comes to your door, can you flex a bit and invite them to stay and eat with you or share a cup of coffee?

The thing about Jesus is he had a reputation for eating and drinking with some "undesirables" (in the eyes of the religious elite, that is; there are no undesirables in God's eyes), and this is powerful.

When we eat food, some good brain chemicals are released. We feel better. When we eat *with others*, we associate with them as pleasant, and a bond is formed.

5. *Plan some helpful and/or fun community events.*

If you have a neighbor whose house is looking a little the worse for wear, organize a one- or two-day community renovation. Once you've gotten to know your neighbors, let the need be known, find out who has skills that are needed, make some work for those with lesser skills (general cleaning, helping, food, and encouragement), take up money, and make the day happen.

You could do the same thing for someone whose car needs some repairs, a poor young couple needing a nursery for their first baby, or an older couple just needing help cleaning the gutters or pressure washing the mold off of their siding. Do not try to do this all on your own; ask for help in order to build community. Others need to help. We were created for the purpose of doing good;[165] by letting others help, you will be helping them.

Or, have a spring festival in your (or someone else's) front yard. You get the idea. Enlist your neighbors to *be neighbors*. Help them learn how to love one another by providing the opportunity.

6. *Share your faith by walking your faith.*

Living purposefully where God has placed you will arouse curiosity. Through this process of being with your neighbors will come the opportunity of showing love (walking in love is the scriptural term) and naturally a chance to be open and winsomely sharing your faith in the Christ.

Sure, you can invite them to church. But perhaps you could (more on this later) have a little *church* in your home. It is part of the original biblical model for the New Covenant "our, not my" believers. And for those who have been hurt or scared off by some of the strange Christian worship traditions, this can be a more natural and acceptable introduction to the faith.

Be on the alert for the previous work God has orchestrated in someone's life. Have circumstances or significant others already laid substantial groundwork? If so, build upon it. Do not be afraid to tell someone whose life is falling apart that they need God and a church family—and share one of the times when you having that made all the difference.

In other words, let's leave behind the catchy and sudden "Did you know you have a hole in your heart the shape of Jesus?" idea and instead just share honestly your love for God in the context of a loving *village life*.

Being Who You Are in Your Calling

Saints of old understood something that perhaps we believers need to be reminded of. *Whatever* it is you are engaged in, for money or not, is something you have been called into. Sure, there are likely some exceptions.

If you are a prostitute, pornographer, or work at an abortion clinic, some restrictions obviously apply. Anything that violates our obligation to love others is *not* something God called you into.

But for those honorable tasks in life, consider that even though you may be miserable or feel out of place (as I did initially in the military), your Creator *placed* you there to be salt and light.

Let's consider some ways your vocation can be a place where the light of the Christ shines.

1. *Be the best at what you do, to the best of your ability.*
   When I was still a fairly new military pilot but had a couple of years' experience, I was wanting to ask my bosses to be promoted from copilot to aircraft commander. I was nervous about asking but sort of felt that I deserved the promotion.

   I ran into a fellow copilot and believer, and he seemed very upset. I asked why, and he stated that he had just asked for the same promotion I wanted—and they flat-out turned him down because, well, he just wasn't that good. He shared his misery with me. He was very dejected.

Internally, although I felt for him, I also saw him as below average in his skills, knowledge, and professionalism. He didn't really seem to put a lot of effort into our profession—so yes, I agreed with him being turned down. He was a slacker. How dare he think he was ready and deserving to be an aircraft commander?

I'm not sure how our Lord does this, but he is really good at it. He gave me a message. I didn't hear an audible voice, there were no spectacular signs in the heavens, but somehow he turned my gaze from my harsh evaluation of my friend to a glaring view of … me.

When I saw a true view of me on the verge of asking my commanders for the same promotion, as I really *was,* I was appalled.

If my brother and friend was a *slacker,* honestly, what term would describe me?

Arrogant?

Foolish?

Lazy?

Entitled?

Wow, that hurt!

I'm so thankful for God's mercy. He stopped me before I embarrassed myself in front of my commanders. I could imagine their response if I had made the request. "You've got to be joking, man. You?"

I was just coasting. I was in no way living by the scripture that admonishes us to "work heartily, as for the Lord and not for men" in spite of my ability to exegete and teach it in a powerful way.

I had already been a civilian pilot when I went to pilot training for the military. My experience made me seem quite talented compared to some of the newbies. I had developed a habit of just *showing up* and thinking that I was impressing people because I was pretty smooth at flying for such a young guy.

Once God corrected me, I had a time of grieving, and I hatched (or the Holy Spirit gave me) a plan.

I would not ask to be promoted to aircraft commander. I would work so hard to become the best that I could be that *they would ask me.* Or I would remain in my current role, as long as I was in the military.

I was prepared to bust my butt for years to become the best I could—because of who I belonged to and who I represented. I had my mind set. This was going to take a while—I had made a pretty bad name for myself.

I went into overdrive studying, being very critical of my flight performance, and seeking direct and harsh feedback on my performance from older pilots.

God had humbled me. I was quiet and not at all impatient. If it took years or never happened, I would endeavor with God's help not to change my intensity.

Six months into this, one of my commanders invited me into his office, closed the door, and looked at me seriously. "Would you be willing to go to aircraft commander upgrade?"

I was stunned.

There's a lesson here from that time period (the early nineties) that is even more true today. Professionalism is so absolutely lacking in nearly every profession that when anyone gets serious about it at all, it gets noticed. Some of your fellow *professionals* will hate you or find you irritating and weird. But quite often, in the "slackidasical" (a word I have for the general type of "professional" today) workforce, those in charge will be drawn to the person who does their work *professionally.*

By the way, do you know what *professionally* means and where it comes from?

It's a word from saints of old. It means to work according to your *profession* that Jesus is Lord. In other words, only *your best effort* is the minimum acceptable way.

Whether you are a woman (or man) staying at home raising children (which is an incorrect thing to say; we never want to *raise children;* we endeavor to *raise adults*—more on that later) or a CEO or a large corporation, you are representing *the Christ*. You can speak all the religious *Jesus words* you want, but no one will hear past how you do what you do every day, and the way you treat everyone in every way.

Endeavor to have whoever you work for to *ask you to accept a promotion* rather than asking for yourself. Or, if your workplace is a bit different, make it impossible for your boss to say no to you.

Of course, in some situations, have the courage to say *no* to a promotion if you perceive the Spirit telling you to say no. Promotions appeal to our perceived need to feel that we are accepted and appreciated, but if the new position will harm your marriage, parenting, or faith, say no.

Which leads us to our next *professional* point.

2. *Be willing to pay the price for doing what is right.*

In my work, it is widely accepted to use sick time to get off from work when you have something better to do. My coworkers talk openly and even joke about it: "Well, that's what sick time is for!"

While doing things according to your profession of faith will generally get you recognized as a leader in your work, it can also draw some friendly fire your way.

I messed up a schedule once at my airline job, quite unintentionally. I basically put myself in a situation, unwittingly, of having to go to work in the middle of a week when I was off because I made an unthinking mistake. When I showed up for that trip, a believer friend and fellow pilot of mine asked what I was doing. When I told him about my mistake, he indeed said, "Hey, that's what sick time is for."

I countered gently, "Well, maybe, but you know as believers we can't call in sick when we are not sick."

He sort of went ballistic on me. "Oh come on. With the way this company treats us, you can't think like that! They screw us over all the time. You have no obligation to them."

I was feeling the heat, but fortunately, his copilot for the day was also a friend and fellow believer, and he chimed in, "No, this is about integrity, boss. You can't be dishonest no matter what the company does."

It got worse, but think about what my second friend said about *integrity*. That is a concept of being together, whole, and in accordance with who you say you are. *Professionalism.*

We represent our Savior wherever we are and in whatever our calling is. The problem I am sharing is nothing new. When Yeshua the Messiah was in a physical body on earth, he saw a guy named Nathanael walking toward him and exclaimed excitedly (note the use of the word "behold," somewhat akin to one of us saying, "Wow, lookie!"), "Behold, an Israelite indeed, in whom there is no deceit!"[166]

Can I rephrase this for you? When Jesus says, *"an Israelite indeed,"* he is to an extent saying, "this guy is *professional!*"

Because, walking as a member of the nation of Israel *without being deceitful* is walking with integrity to the Law. "Thou shalt not lie" is the principle of the profession of the Mosaic Covenant.

Apparently, integrity and professionalism were as rare in Jesus's day as they are in ours.

Be willing to pay the price to earn the surprise that Jesus showed—"Behold! A follower of mine who actually is who they claim to be!"

3.   Be always mindful and prayerful that you are not in your profession for your glorification, profit, or pleasure.

When you do everything to the best of your ability, you'll get a reputation. You may get several reputations. But some will look up to you and admire you, and you will be tempted to protect and even enhance that image.

Do not.

Do. Not.

You are there for a reason, to show the light of the wisdom and love of God to whomever *he* wants that shown to.

Go into your vocation each day prayerfully, that he will show you who or what it is that you need to take care of that day.

If you do that, you will be often surprised. Or delighted. At times, you may end up a bit confused.

In the midst of my being *professional,* I had innumerable surprising moments where our Lord used me—often with me being unaware I was being used.

After a long day of flying, we would end up in military quarters somewhere, tired, and as I relaxed, there would be a knock on the door. As I opened it, one of my crewmembers would walk in with an open Bible and already asking a question. What followed was quite often an in-depth discussion of a deep spiritual challenge this man was facing.

Cool.

Or there was a time when a fellow pilot asked me out to eat. He bought my dinner (at a Burger King in Puerto Rico, elegant dining on his dime!) and began the discussion by asking, "Should I divorce my wife?"

Hmm, seems simple. My answer to him was no.

This is the *confusing* part.

He was dead set on divorce.

We had a good discussion—and he went home and divorced his wife.

To what end was this discussion in my vocation doing the work of God?

I do not know.

I do not have to know.

I was faithful to the moment.

I trust that God was working something in this man's life. My input on it was to the best of my ability representing what scripture teaches. I trust that God continued to work in this friend's life beyond that moment, and I am confident that our Lord accomplished what he wanted through me.

I am not responsible for *results* in my calling. I just have to be faithful to what God puts in front of me.

For you, wherever our God has put you, you must be close to God. Start every morning that you can with him, in his Word, and then walk with the Spirit and be faithful to the people and tasks God places in front of you.

Your calling is to accomplish his purpose. After all, as mentioned in an earlier chapter, a *dead* person doesn't need esteem.

Nothing can top being loved by God and being a new creature working out our covenant mission where you are placed.

The Big-Picture Superhero Life

You have probably figured this out already, but it bears discussing.

The big picture as a blood-bought believer living on this temporary planet goes against popular views of *balance* in various spheres of responsibility.

Some who offer advice on how to live would recommend that you write down all of your various areas of life (i.e., children, spouse, work, recreation, church, etc.) and then try to hit an appropriate amount of time in each area each week.

Totally understandable and completely wrong for the believer.

All of life for the living dead (a.k.a. disciples of Christ) is a matter of seeing every area of life as conducted under the banner of Christ. We love our spouses to Christ. We love our neighbors to his glory. We work hard to represent him in the workplace, to accomplish his goals.

Or, as Jesus put it,

> Therefore I tell you, do not be anxious about your
> life, what you will eat or drink, nor about the body,
> what you will put on. Is not life more than food,
> and the body more than clothing? Look at the birds
> of the air: they neither sow nor reap nor gather into

barns, and yet your heavenly Father feeds them. Are you not of more value than they? And which of you by being anxious can add a single hour to his span of life? And why are you anxious about clothing? Consider the lilies of the field, how they grow: they neither toil nor spin, yet I tell you, even Solomon in all his glory was not arrayed like one of these. But if God so clothes the grass of the field, which today is alive and tomorrow is thrown into the oven, will he not much more clothe you, O you of little faith? Therefore do not be anxious, saying, "What shall we eat?" or "What shall we drink?" or "What shall we wear?" For the Gentiles seek after all these things, and your heavenly Father knows that you need them all. But seek first the kingdom of God and his righteousness, and all these things shall be added to you.[167]

As we noted early on in our time together in this book, fear and anxiety are a natural response to the perils of mortal life on this ball of dirt hurdling through space.

We are redeemed. We are of the Spirit. As is noted by the apostle Paul, to "live is Christ, to die is gain."[168] When our Messiah is telling us not to be anxious, he's just reminding us of the reality of our blessing.

We have had the "riches of his grace lavished upon us."[169] When we look at all the anxious, depressed, sleep-deprived, desperate, addicted, and hopeless people, we must remember that such were we—and we still would be, had not the Christ revealed his great news to us and given us the ultimate life hack: whether we live or die, we're good.

When we see the people mentioned above who do not have this blessing, our hearts should go out to them. Wouldn't our hearts' desire be that they would receive what was freely given to us?

Given the enormous magnitude of the gift given to us, shouldn't our hearts and the Father's heart be one in intent?

Here's the plain truth: the One True Sovereign of the universe has given us the only source of lasting joy and peace. He has given us the hope above all hopes.

Wherever the Almighty has placed you, in your neighborhood or calling, share the glorious inheritance and immeasurably great power that flows from our Father with those he puts in your path.

Dave out ...

CHAPTER 16

Should We Get Political?

One of the penalties for refusing to participate in politics is that
you end up being governed by your inferiors.
—Plato

The darkest places in hell are reserved for those who maintain their neutrality
in times of moral crisis.
—Dante Alighieri

There are many men of principle in both parties in
America, but there is no party of principle.
—Alexis de Toqueville

And Pharaoh said to Joseph, "See, I have set you over all the land of Egypt."
—Genesis 41:41

~~~~~~~~~~~~~~~~~~~~~~~~~

There has been a widespread belief that if only we could
get the right person in the office of the presidency in the
United States, we could bring about the salvation of the nation. Or
perhaps if we can get a majority of believers in Congress, that would
do the trick.

It will not work.

But does that mean believers in the Christ should not seek
political office? Should believers be active in the political process?

Let's look at some important background before we answer.

My Apologies to the Third World

As a young adult traveling the world with the military, I was amazed by two things.

First, the world is a beautiful and fascinating place. There are beautiful and sweet people everywhere—and such a rich diversity of beautiful plants, terrain, and even cities. The people, however, are a testimony to our Creator's love of beauty and to his kindness that resides (potentially) within people all over this planet.

Second, in spite of the beauty of many of the small countries, I did not enjoy being in those places for long. The corruption and cruelty I witnessed in these third world places started at the highest levels and ran all the way down to the local police and even individuals. It was hard to enjoy your travels—you were always on edge, guarding against violence or some sort of trickery.

So I would speak of some corruption I witnessed in politicians in my own country and pronounce, "That's so third world!"

Here lately, I have had to apologize and repent for that.

In my own country and other supposedly *leading* nations of the *first* world, we have shown the world exactly how to be corrupt at a higher level. American government, from local to federal, is now corruption on steroids.

Tyrants of the world, take note. This in the land of the free and home of the brave (well, we used to be) is *the* way to abuse, manipulate, and use people to your own evil desires.

When it comes to corruption, we have the unique and questionable honor of being number one.

The question is, does the child of God have a role to play in this?

Especially given that, as I mentioned earlier, I contend (biblically) that our nation will not be saved solely by a politician or party.

Biblically, a number of God's people did serve in government positions. They were a blessing to the people of their land. Yes, they served in corrupt pagan governments that embraced evil. They made a difference for righteousness in doing so.

They did not save their nation spiritually.

That is a model for us to follow. If we are to be who God says we are, then there are believers (I believe and perceive) who need to step up and serve in political office.

It is an ugly business. It is still the kind of calling that can land you in a fiery furnace or lion's den, just as described in the story of Daniel.

Serving in a government office, elected or appointed, is just a natural extension of the principle of being true to our calling in the last chapter. So perhaps our Lord will place you in a position of running for office or accepting an appointment to serve. If so, serve faithfully. Stand courageously—just as Daniel, Hananiah, Mishael, and Azariah did in previous times. (If you don't recognize the last three names, they are more commonly known by Shadrach, Meshach, and Abednego.)

But perhaps the bigger question is, what is our normal role in the political life of our country?

The Romans 13 Problem

I get challenged on what I am sharing with you in this chapter frequently. The basis of the contention is Romans, chapter 13, where it says,

> Let every person be subject to the governing authorities. For there is no authority except from God, and those that exist have been instituted by God. Therefore, whoever resists the authorities resist what God has appointed, and those who resist will incur judgment.[170]

This seems to be an open-and-shut case for many, and they use examples from the Bible to show, for instance, that the Roman government became quite tyrannical in its ways, and Christians lived under that—without opposition.

Sounds great.

It just isn't true, and those who make such a point are also not aware of the special form of government believers who went before us established, at least in the United States.

The problem with Romans 13 isn't with what it says; it is with the ignorance of those who use it to say that we must obey the government in the United States. If you are in another country, then maybe your governmental documents and form may require obedience.

But in the good ole USA, we have a special kind of problem.

Our governmental heritage goes back primarily to a little-known prerevolution document known as the Fundamental Orders of Connecticut. The believer-citizens of Connecticut wanted to form a government God's way, and so they looked to scripture.

The Orders were built upon a sermon delivered by Reverend Thomas Hooker on May 31, 1638. He proclaimed, using scripture (correctly, I might add), that God granted the people the right to select those who would govern and to proscribe the limits of the power given.

In other words, the Orders were a civil form of a biblical covenant.

In a covenant, a superior establishes the terms, limitations, and even the penalties for the abuse of power. The lesser party either signs on to those terms or refuses to enter the covenant. One normally enters a covenant through a vow, oath, or ceremony.

In the United States Constitution, this same principle is present from the beginning when it states,

> We the people of the United States, in Order to form a more perfect Union, establish Justice, insure domestic Tranquility, provide for the common defence, promote the general Welfare, and secure

the Blessings of Liberty to ourselves and our Posterity, do ordain and establish this Constitution for the United States of America.

Notice that this is *exactly* what Thomas Hooker was proposing. The people (the superior party, with one superior exception) were establishing the *purpose* and *limits* of governmental power. Those powers not given to the government rested with the states, with the individuals, or with one more huge player in this new nation—God himself.

For that, one must go back to the Declaration of Independence.

The role of the Declaration today is not well understood, but it should be understood to not only be a pronouncement of a separation from Great Britain (because she had violated the previous covenants of the Magna Carta and the Englishman's Declaration of Rights), but also it serves as a charter. It declares what this nation is about and what it believes in.

The Declaration specifies that there are certain rights that are inalienable, which means there are things that cannot be taken from the people—among them, life, liberty, and the pursuit of happiness. This is a very radical admission in our world that glorifies man. There is someone above the national ruler, and our petty little elected officials *cannot* change the basic freedoms he grants.

In typical American shallow ways, many do not take the time to study what these rights mean to those who wrote the terms.

For instance, *happiness* in revolutionary times (as in the phrase "pursuit of happiness") was not the current giddy sense of personal euphoria; rather, it was seen as the freedom to pursue what God intended you to do. Sounds a lot like our last chapter. Even though many of the founders were of the noble class, they realized that the concept of restricting certain jobs and roles only to certain people based upon bloodline, financial status, or title was not right in the sight of God.

In the United States at least, when we consider the application of Romans 13, we must remember that those who are representing the federal government only have the power *we* give to them through our covenant, the Constitution. Those powers are limited and few. Even then, what they do must be in recognition of the overarching limits on power—that some rights cannot be messed with, among them, life liberty, and the pursuit of happiness.

The Constitution of the United States and the Fundamental Orders of Connecticut that preceded it by more than two centuries were both radical documents in their day.

But they were actually very old concepts going back to the covenantal process the Father God used with people. It is vital to remember that the one making the covenant is the superior party and defines the terms of the covenant. The parties that sign on or otherwise agree to the covenant do so, it was frequently understood, under the penalty of death.

The oath by which our elected officials enter office (usually and traditionally with their hands on a Bible, swearing before God himself to respect the limits of power) specifies that our Congress members, executive, and judicial branch will uphold the Constitution—*before God.*

In our government this is the way it is supposed to work. Our elected leaders and government service workers are on a short leash. They have agreed to the covenantal restrictions on their power as leaders. In fact, they work for us. If they violate the covenantal restrictions, they are to be removed from office—by force if needed.

This concept was strengthened during the American Civil War when the soldier's oath to "defend the Constitution" was enhanced to include *domestic enemies.* A domestic enemy of the Constitution can be militarily removed from office.

Let us drill down the takeaway from this covenantal and oath principle that we live under. When it comes to Romans 13 and the admonishment to obey government, properly understood in America, we have three basic levels of government.

First, there is God. He has granted certain inalienable

rights—among them life, liberty, and the pursuit of happiness. Once again, make sure you understand what that happiness entails. The Bill of Rights was added because many of the founders did not trust their fellow man to observe the inalienable rights that God had granted to man. They didn't trust those who would govern with this because of the gross violations of these rights by kings and other leaders. They demanded that more of the inalienable things be spelled out.

Would a government forbid churches assembling for worship? The freedom to assemble and freedom of religion were two of the big items that the founders had seen abused in their time under the authority of Great Britain and other nations.

In our time, during the supposed crisis of a "novel" virus with no firm data of its deadliness, government forbade free assembly and constrained free religious expression. As it turns out, COVID-19 had a mortality rate that was likely less than .02 percent, and given that we as believers are free from living in fear (as 1 John 4:6 specifies), why would anyone in the faith be afraid of something like that? Why would we not assemble?

Even if COVID had been something serious, in our faith, our mission does not change because of risk; we who say with the apostle Paul, "To live is Christ and to die is gain,"[171] do not shrink back from loving others or loving God because of a virus.

Further, our constitutionally restrained governments do not have the power to forbid assembly.

But they do so with impunity because of the ignorance of the citizens, as well as through the fear stoked through the governments and their propaganda arm—the media. Just to be clear, if churches went along with these restrictions, even if justified through a false paradigm of loving our neighbors (the lockdowns were more harmful than the disease, as it turns out), then those churches misrepresented our faith. Repentance is in order.

To live in fear of a disease is to walk in darkness. Read 1 John. He is very clear on this.

Here's the point about what we as believers (myself included) should have done (and some did, by the way) when our covenant-limited governments forbade assembling and shut down some businesses. First, we should have shut down the phone lines by calling into government offices for days—demanding that our designated leaders with their limited power *stay within their limited power.*

Sounds drastic and so un-Romans 13. But we need to remember that in America, the limited rights of the government to do *anything* flow from the consent of governed further constrained by our charter (Declaration of Independence) and our Constitution with its Bill of Rights. No emergency should justify such measures. We as a nation choose liberty with all its dangers over "safe" totalitarianism.

As one speaker noted,

> Modern tyranny is terror management. When the terrorist attack comes, remember that authoritarians exploit such events in order to consolidate power. The sudden disaster that requires the end of checks and balances, the dissolution of opposition parties, the suspension of freedom of expression, the right to a fair trial, and so on, is the oldest trick in the Hitlerian book. Do not fall for it.[172]

As members of the superior party of our Constitution, we have an obligation to stay engaged and active with our local, state, and federal governments. It is not optional for an adult believer to participate; it is our duty in respect to the heritage of believers who established this nation to participate. We must demand as the superior party first of all that the inalienable things, those rights that come only from God, are respected.

Secondly, as the superior party, we the people established a body of what was normally called *natural law*—that is, wise principles that limit the power of those who work for us in government.

To be truthful, the Constitution is not terribly long or complex. The principles are few and well established. But if we do not know them, we will not recognize when they are being violated.

As an example, when the *Roe v. Wade* decision was being considered by the Supreme Court to be invalidated, there was a supposed scholarly objection that to invalidate it would violate precedent. Sounds pretty impressive, if you are ignorant.

But what the founders made clear about the Constitution is that an *unconstitutional precedent* would always be unconstitutional no matter how many times it was violated.

Roe v. Wade was, at its core, a spurious coddling of an evil ideology and had no foundation in any principle found in the natural rights of man, especially the "life" provision found in the Declaration of independence.

In the opinion, the court found that there was a right to privacy emanating from the penumbra of the Constitution. So what does that high-sounding finding actually mean?

An *umbra* is a shadow.

Many shadows, depending on the distance from the light source to the illuminated article and then to the surface on which the shadow appears, will have a slightly less shadowy area, and this is the penumbra.

From this shadowy area of the Constitution, claimed the court, something was "emanating." This is stupidity, but no one apparently cared to investigate the big words being used.

Emanate means light or something comes from an object.

A penumbra is a lack of emanation.

Nothing can *emanate* from a shadow.

And of course, if a woman's right to privacy deals with something happening in the womb of a woman, since more than 50 percent of babies are female, the ultimate right to privacy should *prevent* abortion.

Because a baby in the womb is not the woman who is pregnant.

A simple DNA test would prove that. The baby, while in the womb, is not the body of the woman.

The baby has, in America's proclamation of who were are in the declaration of independence, an inalienable right to life, liberty, and the pursuit of happiness.

This is why it is so important for the cause of all that is good and holy that believers keep the command of Jesus when he said we are to *love the Lord our God with all our heart, soul, mind, and strength.*

Being lazy and just going to watch a performance every Sunday will not cut it.

Thirdly, we as believers have an obligation to participate in the state and local levels of government—because the federal side needs to be so limited in its power.

This is a tall order but vital.

How do we do that?

Practical Involvement as Covenantal Citizens

It is important to remember our overarching mission as members of the New Covenant as we endeavor to keep this covenant we know as the United States Constitution. Our mission is to *go into all the world and preach the Gospel.*[173] As it is described in 2 Corinthians, chapters 3 through 6, we have the *ministry of reconciliation.* And in this covenant, we also have the care of one another as admonished in all of the "to one another" passages we discussed earlier.

We must keep all of that in mind, and with that being said, here are some suggestions on being a covenantal citizen:

1. Remember who the enemy is. A brother and sister I love dearly recently shared a powerful story about seeing a social media comment from a young lady following the repeal of the *Roe v. Wade* decision.

This young lady was furious about the decision and was ripping anyone who supported the repeal apart verbally. My friends saw this, contacted a relative, and asked, "Has anyone talked to her?"

Think about that! What is our usual response to someone embracing evil on social media? It is common to blast them as being ungodly, evil, and vile.

My friends, however, saw her as a precious soul made in the image of God, and they knew that there was something going on in her heart that brought out this anger. They called the young woman and invited her over for a meal—and asked gently why she had said what she said.

It was a tragic and heartbreaking story. I'm not at liberty to share details—these things were shared in confidence—but trust that this poor lady had suffered horribly at the hands of a "friend" in a time of need. Abortion had been the "solution" to the problem produced.

Here's the deal. The so-called enemies we may encounter when we attempt to be citizens who advocate for righteousness in governmental affairs are not at all enemies.

They are potential brothers and sisters in Christ, the beloved point of our existence as those who have agreed to the terms of the New Covenant—and they have their reasons for believing what they believe, even if it what they are embracing is an abomination before our God.

We have one enemy, and that is the enemy of our Savior. He captures the hearts and minds of those who strive against what is good and who often hate us for our striving. But we must remember that the prophetic role of Jesus was to "lead captivity captive,"[174] as the old King James put it; in others words, Jesus uses us to show the way out of captivity. Those who believe themselves to be our enemies, unless it is the Satan or one of his demons, are those who have been sadly enslaved to the evil purposes of our Lord.

There is no one-size-fits-all approach to those who are the captives of our true enemy. But perhaps being a good listener and trying to understand why someone believes what they believe is a good start.

Jesus was a friend to the sinners, as the Pharisees noted with disgust. Yes, many of the Pharisees were captives too.

STEPHEN K. MOORE

First principle—*be a gentle friend of those who oppose righteousness. They are captives, not enemies.*

2. *Educate yourself on the Constitution and other governmental forms you live under.* Remember that many fellow believers died to attempt to wrest power away from kings, queens, and other tyrants who would set themselves up as god. They gave us a participatory form of government designed to make it difficult for anyone to do the evil things they had lived under as citizens of their various countries.

The interesting thing is the Constitution is rather simple.

For instance, Congress only has roughly eight specified powers. Much of what is done now is justified under what is termed the "general welfare" clause, which is an abuse of power. "General welfare" has been used to justify governmental regulation and control over a virtually unlimited spectrum of topics. Why would the authors of the Constitution impose specific limits on Congress if they were then unlimited by the concept of general welfare?

Presidential power (the executive branch) has been sorely abused for decades, if not a century or more. The executive branch only has the normative power to ensure that the laws passed by Congress are faithfully carried out. Any executive order must directly relate to a proper law (within the eight delineated powers) of Congress. Recently, President Joe Biden issued an executive order regarding student loan forgiveness. It is unrelated to any lawful aspect of congressional power (there is no federal authority delegated under the Constitution as pertaining to education—that is a state or local issue, or personal), and further, it is nothing more than a vote-buying act of financial irresponsibility that encourages childishness in the populace.

It must be opposed by the believer as a member of the covenantal agreement.

Another grievous example of the abuse of power has been the congressional power to declare war. It is firmly noted in James Madison's notes on the Constitution that the initial wording was that Congress had the power to "make war," and this was changed to "declare war." This was because the founders knew that greedy influences in powerful circumstances benefit from war *making*, and so it was intended that Congress had to have a discussion, take input from those they work for (that would be *us*; i.e., do we see the cause of war as justifying the deaths of our sons and daughters? If not, then we as citizens say no to the declaration), and then make a formal *declaration* of war if the *people whom they work for feel jugular enough to do so.*

The president cannot send us to war; he can only respond to the immediate phase of an attack against our nation until Congress can meet.

In the War Powers Act of 1973, this power of the executive was supposedly clarified, but this has proved to be problematic and unconstitutional. Like many spurious and illegal laws, the War Powers Act has resulted in presidents basically making war within the thirty-day restriction on such actions specified by the act, and then Congress making a nonbinding resolution of agreement later.

Or in the case of President Barack Obama and the Libyan war action, the Constitution was utterly disregarded as well as the War Powers Act. The president ordered us into war for more than the unconstitutional War Power Act limit of thirty days. Congress never challenged him. Our military officers did not challenge him either, likely due to their lack of knowledge of the document they took an oath to defend.

The point here is not to criticize former presidents, Congress, and military officers; rather, it is to point out that the citizens of the United States have forsaken their role in this covenantal process. Our governmental school system (a.k.a. the public schools) do not train us as young people to be good participatory and educated citizens; they instead teach us to go along with whatever the government wants.

Second principle—*educate yourself and your family on the Constitution and your state/local governmental forms. Participate fully in the process as a citizen. Fellow believers fought and died to preserve this right for you.*

3. *Love the Lord with all your* mind *in this process of being a citizen. Be courageous and not anxious.* Learn to think. It is a hard business that can be very unsettling. One of my other highest recommended books is *Thinking Fast and Slow* by Daniel Kahneman.[175] It's another life-changing book, but just to summarize and totally butcher the book (it is truly excellent), we humans do not think well, even those in the thinking professions. We tend to believe things with very little thought and do not properly sort things out to see what is true and just.

When Jesus was asked about the greatest commandment in the law, he quoted Deuteronomy but expanded it just a bit in an important way:

> You shall love the Lord your God with all your heart
> and with all your soul and with all your mind.[176]

"Your mind" was the important addition. Likely a nod to the Greek emphasis on reason and thought, this clarifies the wholeness of the *soul* in Hebrew terms, which would include your thinking abilities.

We need to stop ignoring Jesus in this area and learn to think through what we hear before we believe anything. As I mentioned in my earlier book, *Thrive: The Biblical Essential of Conquering Trauma and Being Resilient,*[177] too many believers are de facto cult members, because they believe what they have heard from others that sounds good to them. They have invested little or no effort into what they believe; they have just gone with that which makes them feel good.

Read the book *Thinking Fast and Slow* mentioned above. It is the best work on thinking I had read to date. It is a life-changing book.

4. If the political process is of special interest to you, become a specialist for your "our, not my" church. It is not practical for everyone to be experts on the constitutional covenant or to monitor what is happening politically on a national, state, and local level. But if this does interest you, join with a few like-minded folks in your church family (and work with other church families in your area) to help inform people of the important issues being processed by our public servants, the stance on righteousness taken by those running for office, and any nefarious law-making activities that require opposition.

In doing so, make use of groups such as Second Vote and any number of organizations that work to do this on a large scale. (Second Vote analyzes the corporate policies of companies and highlights those who promote ungodly agendas—so the righteous can better know where to spend their money.)

As military units have soldiers that specialize in particular parts of the mission (demolition, sharpshooting, communication, medical, etc.), so must our offensive units for the kingdom also have specialists. We depend on one another. If our Lord has given you a heart for the political process, get busy and lead the way!

Dave out ...

CHAPTER 17

The Wrap-Up—The God Who Loves Village Life

In the days of Shamgar, son of Anath, in the days of Jael, the highways were abandoned, and travelers kept to the byways. The villagers ceased in Israel; they ceased to be until I arose; I, Deborah, arose as a mother in Israel.
—Deborah, the judge

It is undeniable that religion has played a major role in every period of civic revival in American history.
—Robert Putnam

When one tugs at a single thing in nature, he finds it attached to the rest of the world.
—John Muir

Exile from the tribe is a form of execution.
—Richard Paul Evans

~~~~~~~~~~

The story of the judge, Deborah, found in the Old Testament book of Judges, has been misused a lot.

But the simple message is this.

God cares that village life flourishes.

That's why he has always brought people together. That's why he called Deborah, a woman leader when women didn't do that, when the men of her village were cowering in fear. His heart was that village life would resume, because living *together* and connected is what is best for his children—and we are all his children, though some are away in a far country.

The first institution he created once the world was finished was *marriage,* and from that stems the family.

He entrusted the mission of bringing the Messiah and thus salvation to all—not to an individual or a country but to a *family.*

He established his church, *the household of God,*[178] in which its family members are to be deeply interdependent on one another—keeping the "to one another" admonitions we spoke of earlier.

We can confidently infer, as our Lord God has never changed,[179] that his heart is still aching that all of his children (even the wayward and rebellious ones) live with lots of people around them to love and be loved by.

In short, our Creator wants healthy village life to be the norm.

One Very Practical Aspect of Village Life

A young friend sent me an interactive display (through social media) of the wealth of then Amazon CEO Jeff Bezos. It was stunning. This guy has more money than many nations' gross domestic products put together. This presentation brought up a concern that I do share—too much wealth in the hands of too few people tends to be problematic.

Personally, I have observed that the super wealthy lose touch with the humanity of the average human being. They become cold and inhumane, although they are careful to present themselves as philanthropic. Their philanthropy is based upon an overestimation of their own intellect and an embracing of relativistic ideologies that do not respect the image of God present in *every* person, whereas the wealthy are the most likely to embrace the need of population control—and of course certain types of people are always targeted by them for extinction.

But this infographic my friend sent me suggested the solution

251

was that "the government should take a percentage of Bezos's wealth and distribute it," as only an all-knowing and beneficent government could.

Having worked full-time for the United States government for a number of years, I knew this was an utterly ignorant idea.

Here's the big question about Bezos:

Who created Bezos and his wealth?

The correct answer is *me*.

And *you*.

I was an early adopter of Amazon, first as an easy way to order books from home and then eventually almost everything else. The number of old Amazon boxes in my garage at times became absurd.

It was convenient. I didn't think that I liked going to town to shop. It seemed to save money and time.

It was, in fact, a betrayal of my village and healthy social connections.

There is a village way to get the things you need, although much of it has been destroyed by the success of big-box stores, Amazon, and other online retailers.

As for books, there is a great local independent bookstore in my little town called Reading Rock bookstore. They can order any book I want and usually have it for me within two days.

But even better, when I walk into the store, Angela (the owner), or Rachel, or Phyllis, or whoever is working will say, "Oh hi, Steve!" We catch up on what has been going on, what each of us is reading, and so forth. While many times our conversations are just casual and pleasant, as I have gotten to know these members of my town (and they me), sometimes there is a much deeper conversation that takes place. These are the moments when deep spiritual issues can be brought to the fore, deeper connection and trust is established, and the work of the kingdom of Christ can be advanced.

We are part of our village, our community, for a reason.

We used to have a local building-supply place run by my good friend Henry. When I was working on a project (and I am an amateur), I could go in, tell Henry what I was trying to do, and he would tell me and even *pull* what I needed. He would give me instructions on how to use what I bought.

The big-box building-supply store moved into our little town. Henry went out of business. The worker bees in the big-box store can sometimes help, but the turnover is high, and most of them don't know much about building. Our community can save a few dollars at the big store, but was it worth the trade-off of the close relationships that had been in place for decades under the old local ownership of nearly every type of business?

There are lots of chain food places in our little town, with worker bees.

There are also local places. I have, in an endeavor to support village life just like God does, largely restricted my business to local places. I learn the names of those who own and work there as much as I can. It is part of developing what author Wendell Berry calls *membership.*

In his novels *Jayber Crow*[180] and *Hannah Coulter,*[181] the stories take place in a place called Port William. Anyone who lives there is part of the "Port William membership." Berry is not only a writer but a philosopher, and he believes strongly in the value of close relationships, the importance of local ownership of stores, schools, and strong interdependence of community members. His novels show in beautiful ways the importance of the village where everyone pulls together, lives at a slower pace, and cares for the world in which we live.

I highly recommend these two novels.

The point here is that we really need to do what God showed was on his heart in that old story of Deborah.

The world, with its insatiable desire for more profit, power, and efficiency, is ruining the social structures that were put in place by God himself.

Given that we as his children were put here on earth to *tend his garden,* shouldn't we be the leaders in our communities in doing so?

Let us show the world a better way.

Undoing the Mass Delusion through the Beauty of God's Love

As we noted early on, there are atrocious ideologies being embraced by a significant percentage of the global society. They are nothing truly new—just repackaged and renamed variants of the old ideas that led to the deaths of millions of people at the hands of their neighbors in the twentieth century alone.

We, the "our, not my" household of God, have the antidote to this heinous isolation and dangerous anger in the world today.

We, like Deborah and her compatriots, need to stand and provide the picture of loving village life as God intended.

It starts in our churches (as the body, not the building) and continues wherever God puts us.

Whether we are at work, at home, or walking through our neighborhood, we need to exude love for all—just as Jesus did.

Joshua, the common laborer of Nazareth, a.k.a. Jesus, hung out with everyone. From the very religious Pharisee to the prostitutes and IRS agents (tax collectors), he could be found eating, laughing, touching, and talking.

He was the draw to the life of God's village.

He still is.

He lives in us.

Let us live beautifully to restore village life.

Dave out …

aPPENDIX

Un-Hacking Your Life Program—
Taming the Digital Dragon

The following guide is one from one of my seminars on getting free from digital distraction. It is the process I developed for myself when I realized I was wasting my life on unworthy garbage.

While it is specifically designed for electronic devices, television, video games, and social media distractions, it is easy to apply to sugar, food, or other habituated comforts (addictions, if you prefer).

For instance, you have to decide what you *will* eat instead of sugar, if you are trying to rid your life of that toxin. You need social support and healthy activities anytime you are trying to kick old, harmful habits to the curb.

Let this be a starting framework for any time and life wasters you have in your life.

Step 1: The Vital Electronic Media Planner

Problem: Undefined, unnecessary, and low-value electronic media and devices steals our time, harm our relationships, and are *usually addictive in nature.* In preparation for breaking the addiction cycle, determine and write down what activities are *essential* for you that involve electronic media, especially on a smartphone. *Essential* means that if this task is not accomplished, serious relational, health, education, or vocational consequences will follow. Unless you currently earn a living playing video games, games are not essential.

Solution: Defining what you *must* do during the six-week electronic media detox will empower you to break the addictive cycle of unplanned electronic media use and eliminate the temptation of going back to old habits. This *essential* usage mindset will form the foundation of your future use of technology.

Transformational benefit: Defining only what you must do will help you eliminate distraction and empower you to gain control over your tech usage. This is a vital step in the six-week detox process.

These are my essential activities on a smartphone:

Essential activities on a tablet or laptop/desktop:

Step 2: The Healthy Pleasure Planner

Problem: Simply trying to *stop* a bad habit rarely works. It tends to increase our focus on what we do not want to do, which leads to relapses in undesired behaviors.

Solution: Choosing healthy and emotionally/spiritually nourishing activities that we *will do* during the six-week detox gives us something to reach for when we feel a need to reach for our old habits. Here are a list of some healthy activities that produce joy, connection, and relaxation:

- playing/singing/listening to music
- playing board games, card games, or group sports
- bike riding, walking, or other physical activities, especially with friends or family
- being out in nature (hiking, camping, relaxing in a *green*, natural environment)
- reading a real book (the Bible, good nonfiction, great fiction)
- reflecting on life or what you have read or are struggling with
- getting together with friend(s), either having people over or meeting somewhere
- calling a friend, just to reconnect
- taking a nap
- praying
- joining a community organization (church, choir, bowling league, civic club, etc.)
- volunteering to help others

Transformational benefits: Deciding to routinely engage in emotionally/spiritually/relationally healthy activities will fill the void left by your former addictive media—but in a way that increases your well-being and is in alignment with what you value most in life.

Activities I will engage in. For the next six weeks (and beyond), what will I *determine to do* that will satisfy my need for pleasure and joy that is good for me emotionally, spiritually, and relationally?

Step 3: Deep Abilities Planner

Problem: Addictive electronic media prevents personal growth—period. The very nature of the short-term dopamine reward cycle keeps us agitated, distracted, and unable to concentrate. Deep reading and reflection are essential to personal growth in wisdom, contentment, and abilities. The current overuse of addictive apps, social media, email, notifications, pull-to-refresh, video games, streaming videos, binge-watching television, televised sports, and video games is creating an unwise and immature populace.

Solution: An intentional commitment and plan to develop or redevelop deep reading capabilities and the choice to spend time in quiet reflection will increase our peace, maturity, wisdom, and overall capabilities to be successful in life.

Transformation benefits: Deep reading activates every level of our brains, exponentially enhances our learning and wisdom, increases our attention span, and brings joy. Time spent in reflection allows us to further increase in wisdom, to achieve peace with the problems in our lives, and to stay focused on what we value the most.

Make a reading list of books you will read over the six-week detox period. (Some suggested books are listed below.)

Suggested Reads:

Crazy Love by Francis Chan
None Greater by Matthew Barrett
Love the Lord with All Your Mind by Moreland
Prodigal God by Keller
The Gospel Comes with a House Key by Butterfield
A Mind for God by White

Openness Unhindered by Butterfield
Letters to the Church by Chan
The Prayer of Jesus by Hanegraaff
7 Women and the Secret of Their Greatness by Metaxas
The Secret Thoughts of an Unlikely Convert by Butterfield
The Olivet Discourse Made Easy by Gentry
The Divine Conspiracy by Willard
The Destruction of Jerusalem by Holford
The Screwtape Letters by Lewis
Seeking Allah, Finding Jesus by Qureshi
Celebration of Discipline by Foster
The Apocalypse Code by Hanegraaff
Not a Fan by Idleman
Renovation of the Heart by Willard
Radical by Platt
Sacred Parenting by Thomas
The Knowledge of the Holy by Tozier
Playing with Fire by Russell

Good Reads—Secular:

Man's Search for Meaning by Frankl
Irresistible by Alter
Signature in the Cell by Meyer
Reader Come Home by Wolf
Bowling Alone by Putnam
Sexual Sabotage by Reisman
How Evil Works by Kupellian
The Shallows: What the Internet Is Doing to Our Brains by Carr
The Coddling of the American Mind by Lukianoff, Haidt
The Narcissism Epidemic by Twenge
The Hacking of the American Mind by Lustig
Glow Kids by Kardaras

Good Reads—Fiction:

1984 by Orwell
Jane Eyre by Bronte
A Tale of Two Cities by Dickens
Brave New World by Huxley
Adventures of Sherlock Holmes by Conan-Doyle
Les Miserable by Hugo
Fahrenheit 451 by Bradbury
Animal Farm by Orwell
The Giver by Lowry
The Book Thief by Zusak
Anna Karenina by Tolstoy
The Brothers Karamazov by Dostoyevsky
The Little Prince by de Saint-Exupery
Moby Dick by Melville
One Day in the Life of Ivan Denisovich by Solzhenitsyn
To Kill a Mockingbird by Lee
Pride and Prejudice by Austen
The Lion, the Witch, and the Wardrobe by Lewis
The Screwtape Letters by Lewis
The Hobbit by Tolkien

Steps to developing deep reading (if you are not currently a deep reader): It is best to set aside a minimum of twenty minutes in which you will read the book you have selected without distraction. If you have not been in the habit of reading, this will be difficult, but stick with it. Try to read deeply for at least twenty minutes at a time, twice a day. If possible, take five to ten minutes to think about the implications of what you have just read, as if you were going to share what you learned with someone else.

Try to gradually increase your reading time during the six-week period. If you are a busy mom, let the children see you reading and make it clear that "this is mommy's reading time; go entertain yourself or I can give you a chore to do." They need to see your example, and they also need to learn to keep themselves busy.

Warning: This may be a real struggle, but it is so worth it! Reading develops empathy, attention span, wisdom, knowledge, and inner peace. Do not give up in developing your deep reading abilities!

Developing a habit of solitude/reflection: One of the reasons we reach for social media, a game, email, or video is that we are emotionally hurting, conflicted, insecure, or fearful—often because we have not taken the time to deal mentally with the important but painful realities in our life. It is vital to our peace, health, and to breaking our media addiction to establish the habit of sitting quietly and reflecting on what is happening within us and around us.

For those of you who are Christians, this is often best done in your morning time with God. I call this my armor-up time, and I see it as a personal encounter with the Holy Spirit and Jesus. It is a time to listen to them through the Word, to speak to them, and to pay attention to any turmoil within my heart. It is *vital* that we learn to reflect on life in order to achieve peace—and to achieve victory over life-stealing electronic media.

At what times of day will I read?

At what time of day will I engage in reflection?

I will carry a real book with me wherever I go for six weeks.

Step 4: The People Connection Planner

Problem: Addictive electronic media prevents loving connection with others. In our always connected environment, Americans are lonelier and more depressed, anxious, and tired than ever.

Solution: We were designed to connect deeply and share our lives with others. It is essential to our well-being that we are face-to-face and side by side, sharing life, food, joy, sorrow, and wisdom with others on a regular basis. We must make meeting up with others a priority each week and also belong to groups that provide for friendship and common activities.

Transformational benefits: Deep and meaningful relationships have proven essential in obtaining freedom from addictions. Family, friends, and belonging to groups with a common values bring emotional, physical, and spiritual health to us.

List ten people you will deepen your relationship with during the six-week detox.

Specifically, how do you plan to connect and nurture the relationship with each person (i.e., have them over, call them, meet for coffee, take a trip together, have a game night)?

Put this on your calendar, specifically when will you contact them and try to get together.

If you are not already a member of at least two community groups, what group(s) will you join during the six-week detox? (Suggested groups: churches, choir, bowling league, civic organization, charitable group.)

Step 5: Plan Your Peace

Problem: Addictive electronic media prevents loving connection with others. In our always connected environment, Americans are lonelier, more depressed, anxious, and tired than ever.

Solution: We were designed to connect deeply and share our lives with others. It is essential to our well-being that we are face-to-face and side by side, sharing life, food, joy, sorrow, and wisdom with others on a regular basis. We must make meeting up with others a priority each week and also belong to groups that provide for friendship and common activities.

Transformational benefits: Deep and meaningful relationships have proven essential in obtaining freedom from addictions. Family, friends, and belonging to groups with a common values bring emotional, physical, and spiritual health to us.

List ten people you will deepen your relationship with during the six-week detox.

Specifically, how do you plan to connect and nurture the relationship with each person (i.e., have them over, call them, meet for coffee, take a trip together, have a game night)?

Put this on your calendar, specifically when will you contact them and try to get together.

If you are not already a member of at least two community groups, what group(s) will you join during the six-week detox? (Suggested groups: churches, choir, bowling league, civic organization, charitable group.)

Step 6: Defang Your Dragon

Problem: Our smartphones are usually our biggest challenge; because they are portable and within reach, it is too easy to fall back into old time- and life-wasting behaviors.

Solution: For at least the period of the six-week detox, remove all nonessential apps from your phone (i.e., social media, messaging apps other than basic texting, games, or any other app that you have determined uses a lot of your time). It is important to, as much as possible, reduce your phone to just a very basic communication device during this period. You can always reinstall apps after the six weeks is over if you determine you need it and can control your usage.

Transformational benefits: You get your life back, or perhaps have a real life for the first time ever. Without this little handheld god controlling you, you can begin to live your life in accordance with your values. You can build real relationships, deepen your wisdom and peace, and improve your health, happiness, joy, and contentment.

What apps take up most of your time and are not essential?

Delete them from your smartphone.

Turn off all notifications on your smartphone.

If you are a gamer, get whatever device you use out of your house or control. Let any partners know you are unavailable to play for the next six weeks—and hopefully forever.

Advanced (but so worth it): Get rid of Netflix, Hulu, Roku, or other streaming services. Get rid of cable or satellite TV. You can get free videos and somewhat older TV series from the library. You can watch sports in season at the local high school, which is social. You will save a lot of money and regain even more of the good life.

Step 7: Start the Six-Week Digital Detox/Fast

Problem: We are trapped in a dopamine reward cycle with our electronic media, apps, and devices. It is stealing our lives, ruining our relationships, and making us the most tired, anxious, depressed, and lonely generation in the history of the world. But it is based upon addictive habits, and these habits are hard to break. We must now step away from electronic media to the max extent possible and choose to engage in healthy and contentment-producing behaviors in order to build a new way of life.

Solution: Break the old habits through a disciplined six-week plan of fasting from addictive technology and engaging in healthy connection, deep reading / reflection, and healthy pleasures.

Transformational benefits: You begin to live your life in accordance with what is truly important to you, in a way that produces contentment, joy, and health.

Pick the day on which the six-week fast/detox will begin.

Make sure you have completed your plan by finishing the previous six lessons.

Begin the fast. Mark on your calendar(s) the start and projected end date.

Helpful tips:

- Decide in advance if you will watch any TV. Only watch what you intend to (no binge-watching), and preferably watch with someone else (use this time as a people connection, enjoy the show together).

- Do not use any light-emitting device within two hours of going to bed.
- Do not keep any device in your bedroom. Keep it out of sight, out of hearing.
- If you have trouble sleeping, do not use an electronic device. Read a real book in calming yellow/orange light (not too bright) or spend time in prayer/reflection.
- Turn off your Wi-Fi within two hours of bedtime. If you have children, have a place where they can charge their devices but not have access to them. Do not allow them to have any computer in their rooms.
- Do not have a smartphone out, visible, or making noise while you are connecting with others.
- You may relapse; do not quit. Just pick it up again. Seek support and encouragement. There may be some really deep issues driving you back into comfort-seeking behaviors.
- Seek to develop a healthy lifestyle during this fast. Seek to truly connect, eat well, exercise, recapture a sense of wonder at the world, enjoy nature, enjoy music, and enjoy your Creator.
- Try to continually grow, learn, and adapt during this forty-day fast.

Wrap-up: You will learn much during this time. You may wish to extend the fast or even try to defeat any other addictions (such as unhealthy foods) after this area is conquered. Go for it. And share this with friends who are struggling, but let them move at their own pace.

Please share your feedback with me during and after the process. If you find ideas that really helped you that might help others, please email them to me at skmoore63@comcast.net.

Bonus: Tips for Parents

1. When should I get my child a smartphone? Never.

2. Should my child have their own tablet/laptop? Perhaps, depending on the maturity of the child. But it needs to be in full control of the parents. It is to be issued to the child for specific tasks at specific times and used in a family area, never in private. If Steve Jobs wouldn't let his children have an iPad, why would we?

3. Should my child be allowed to play video games? There is an argument that this increases coordination and brain-processing speed, but so does biking, kickball, softball, roller blading, and so on. Generally speaking, use caution about ever introducing this. Let them ruin their own life later. If you do allow it, I would suggest only allowing an hour or two on the weekends if all schoolwork and chores have been done.

4. What are some important things I need to ensure my child receives?
    a. Unstructured play time.
    b. Increasing responsibility and freedom with age (no helicopter parenting).
    c. Regular social connection with all ages of people.
    d. Make trips to the library or local bookstore a big and weekly event.
    e. Have meals together and have your children share what they are reading. Encourage them to use full and proper English. Ask many thought questions to drive them back to the book.
    f. Have real and meaningful chores that help the family to function.
    g. Avoid excess organized sports activities. Local, child-organized games are better and more maturing.

h. Set the example.

i. Disable Wi-Fi access at night and have a secure place to store devices that no one will access from two hours prior to bed until absolutely needed the next day.

5. If your child is already an electronic media junkie, a detox will be necessary. This will usually not be accepted with enthusiasm. Professional help may be required, depending on the severity of the addiction.

6. Keep good books around the house and set the example of restraint with electronics and reading. Have people of all ages over on a regular basis and make sure your kids are right in the middle of this. They must learn to interact with all age levels.

7. Schedule your child for age-appropriate service projects. Helping with local charities, local widows or widowers, church projects, mission trips, and serious camps (such as Summit ministries) will give them opportunities to mature.

Copyright 2019 by Stephen K. Moore

ENDNOTES

1   I.X. Kendi, quoted in *New York Post* article, "BU Professor Ripped After He Implies Amy Coney Barrett Is a 'White Colonizer,'" January 20, 2022, retrieved from https://nypost.com/2020/09/28/bu-professor-suggests-amy-coney-barrett-is-a-white-colonizer/.

2   Ibid.

3   C. Browning, *Ordinary Men: Reserve Police Battalion 101 and the Final Solution in Poland,* revised edition (HarperCollins Publishers, 2017). This book is one of several studies of how ordinary citizens not only took part in the atrocities of Nazi Germany but excelled in doing so.

4   Information taken from interview with Professor Mattias Desmet found at https://www.peakprosperity.com/mattias-desmet-on-mass-formation/.

5   Retrieved from https://mcc.gse.harvard.edu/reports/loneliness-in-america.

6   See https://www.ncbi.nlm.nih.gov/pmc/articles/PMC7441973/.

7   Phil. 2:3.

8   1 Jn. 4:4.

9   1 Jn. 4:18.

10 Mt. 16:18.

11 Rom. 11:3

12 Rom. 11:4

13 Rom. 2:1

14 Gal. 6:2

15 In late 2021, the CDC changed their definitions of a vaccination from providing *immunity* to instead providing *protection*. However, their definition as of review date September 1, 2021, is still problematic and contradictory. They claim *immunity* is protection from an infectious disease and that "if you are immune to a disease, you can be exposed and not infected." While their revised definition of a vaccine providing

271

"protection" would cause the mRNA vaccines to be a "vaccine," their definition of immunity contradicts the mRNA being able to be classified as such—for they fail to prevent infection. Definitions retrieved from https://www.cdc.gov/vaccines/vac-gen/imz-basics.htm on January 27, 2022.

[16] Desai et.al, 2021, *Can SARS-CoV-2 vaccine increase the risk of reactivation of Varicella zoster? A systematic review,* retrieved from: https://onlinelibrary.wiley.com/doi/full/10.1111/jocd.14521 See also *Whistleblowers Share DOD Medical Data that Blows Vaccine Safety Debate Wide Open* at https://truthpress.news/news/whistleblowers-share-dod-medical-data-that-blows-vaccine-safety-debate-wide-open/

[17] https://dpbh.nv.gov/uploadedFiles/dpbhnvgov/content/Boards/BOH/Meetings/2021/SENEFF-1.PDm

[18] https://doi.org/10.3389/fmed.2021.798095

[19] 1 Jn. 1:5

[20] Jn. 10:10

[21] Ibid.

[22] Ibid.

[23] Ibid.

[24] Phil. 4:7

[25] S. Junger, *Tribe: On Homecoming and Belonging,* 2016, Fourth Estate, London.

[26] Heb. 2:14, 15

[27] 2 Cor. 5:6–9

[28] B. Webb & J.D. Mann, *Mastering Fear: A Navy Seal's Guide,* 2018, Penguin Random House, LLC, New York.

[29] L. Gonzales, *Deep Survival: Who Lives, Who Dies, and Why,* 2003, W.W. Norton & Company, New York

[30] Ibid, p. 136

[31] Psalm 90:12

[32] S.Moore, *Thrive: The Biblical Essential of Conquering Trauma and Being Resilient,* 2022, Workbook Press.

[33] Mal. 3:6

[34] Mal. 2:17

[35] Ex. 33:18

[36] Ex. 33:19, 20

[37] Jn. 5:19

[38] 1 Jn. 3:1–3

[39] Jn. 6:68

272

40 A. Alter, *Irresistible: The Rise of Addictive Technology and the Business of Keeping Us Hooked,* Penguin Press, New York, 2017.

41 Ibid, p. 137

42 Data retrieved from https://sugarscience.ucsf.edu/dispelling-myths-too-much.html

43 R.H. Lustig, M.D., *The Hacking of the American Mind,* 2017, Penguin Random House, New York.

44 Ibid.

45 P. Graham, *The Acceleration of Addictiveness,* 2010, PaulGraham.com.

46 John 10:10

47 P. Graham, *The Acceleration of Addictiveness,* 2010, PaulGraham.com.

48 N. Carr, *The Shallows: What the Internet is Doing to Our Brains,* W.W. Norton & Co., 2010, New York.

49 Ibid, p. 1.

50 Jn. 6:1–15

51 Jn. 6:15

52 Gen. 2:2, 3

53 Ex. 20:8, 9

54 Jn. 4:32

55 Col. 3:23

56 Lk. 16:10

57 M. Wolf, *Proust and the Squid: The Story and Science of the Reading Brain,* 2007, Harper Perennial, New York.

58 Mt. 15:21–28

59 Ez. 18:1–4

60 Ez. 18:25

61 Ez. 18:19

62 Is. 5:20, 21

63 Mt. 26:11

64 T. Sowell, *Black Rednecks and White Liberals,* Encounter Books, 2005, NY.

65 Ibid, p. 6.

66 Ibid, p. 43

67 V.E. Frankl, *Man's Search for Meaning,* 2006, Beacon Press, Boston, MA.

68 V.E. Frankl, *Man's Search for Meaning,* 2006, Beacon Press, Boston, MA.

69 K.A. April, B. Dharani, K. Peters, *Impact of Locus of Control Expectancy on Level of Well-Being,* 2012, doi:10.5539/res.v4n2p124

70 Mk. 12:29–31

71 Heb. 12:5, 6

72 Heb. 12:12–15

73 Neh. 1:6, 7
74 Brandeis University. *Medicalizing human conditions: A growth industry— but what does it cost?* Science Daily, 19 May 2010. Retrieved from www.sciencedaily.com/releases/2010/05/100517152536.htm
75 Ibid.
76 H.G. Welch. *The medicalization of life.* Los Angeles Times, 15 March, 2010. Retrieved from https://www.latimes.com/archives/la-xpm-2010-mar-15-la-oe-welch15-2010mar15-story.html
77 Gen. 1:31
78 Ps. 73:1–8
79 Ps. 73:16–22
80 Mt. 16:18
81 1 Pet. 2:9
82 2 Corinthians, chapters 2 through 5, contain a thorough discussion of our covenantal mission to engage in the reconciliation of lost sinners to their Creator.
83 2 Cor. 10:3–6
84 Mt. 22:37
85 D. Inserra, *Getting Over Yourself: Trading Believe-In-Yourself Religion for Christ-Centered Christianity,* 2021, Moody, Chicago
86 1 Sam. 17:34
87 1 Sam. 22:1, 2
88 1 Cor. 12:13–20
89 2 Sam. 7:18–22
90 Mt. 15:25
91 2 Sam. 24:1, 2
92 2 Sam. 24:3
93 Rom. 12:1
94 Eph. 1:7
95 Acts 3:1
96 Jsh. 7:3
97 Jsh. 7:3, 4
98 Jsh. 7:7
99 Jsh. 7:10, 11
100 Rom. 3:23
101 Jsh. 7:10
102 Mt. 6:1
103 Dr. Bryan McAlister, I love this guy!
104 1 Jn. 4:18, 19

105 Is. 53:2

106 Phil. 2:5–8

107 Phil. 1:27

108 Phil. 2:1, 2

109 Phil. 2:3–7

110 Mt. 6:1

111 Mt. 5:3

112 Jn. 15:1–13

113 https://mcc.gse.harvard.edu/reports/loneliness-in-america

114 Ibid.

115 Ibid.

116 Ibid.

117 Ibid.

118 Eph. 1:7, 8.

119 Mt. 7:1–14

120 Acts 5:42

121 Gal. 6:1, 2.

122 Phil. 2:3–8

123 Gal. 2:20

124 S.Junger, *Tribe: On Homecoming and Belonging,* 2016, Hachette Book Group.

125 Ibid.

126 D. Bonhoeffer, *The Cost of Discipleship,* 1995, Touchstone.

127 Rom. 5:8

128 Pro. 18:24

129 Acts 5:42

130 Rom. 6:3, 4

131 2 Cor. 3:5–18, excerpts.

132 Ibid, 5:11

133 R. Champagne Butterfield, *The Gospel Comes with a House Key: Practicing Radically Ordinary Hospitality in our Post-Christian World,* 2018, Crossway, Wheaton Il.

134 Ibid, 5:15

135 Mt. 6:24

136 Ibid. 6:33

137 2 Cor. 3:5, 6

138 Ibid. 5:16

139 Acts 17:26

140 Ibid. 5:18, 19

141   2 Cor. 5:19

142   Ibid.

143   Ibid. 5:20, 21

144   1 Sam. 17:45

145   Retrieved from https://www.preceptaustin.org/shalom_-_definition

146   Jn. 14:27

147   Jn. 15:1–11

148   Titus 3:4–7

149   Ps. 111:10

150   Eph. 5:25–32

151   1 Jn. 3:16–18

152   Mt. 26:36–39

153   1 Cor. 6:9–11

154   1 Cor. 6:7

155   Mt. 11;19

156   G. Koukl, 2019, Zondervan, Grand Rapids.

157   1 Jn. 1:5

158   Jdg. 5:6, 7

159   Ibid., vv. 15–17

160   Ibid., vv. 2, 18

161   M. Desmet, *The Psychology of Totalitarianism,* 2022, Chelsea Green Publishing, Vermont, p. 42

162   Ibid.

163   Ibid.

164   R. Champagne Butterfield, *The Gospel Comes with a House Key: Practicing Radically Ordinary Hospitality in Our Post-Christian World,* 2018, Crossway, IL, p. 78.

165   Ephesians 2:10

166   Jn. 1:47

167   Mt. 6:25–33

168   Phil. 1:21

169   Eph. 1:7, 8

170   Rom. 13:1, 2

171   Phil. 1:21

172   T. Snyder, retrieved from https://www.litcharts.com/lit/on-tyranny/symbols/emergencies

173   Mk. 16:13

174   Eph. 4:8

[175] D. Kahneman, *Thinking Fast and Slow,* Farrar, Straus, and Giroux, 2011, New York

[176] Mt. 22:37

[177] 2022, Workbook Press Publishing.

[178] Eph. 2:19

[179] Mal. 3:6

[180] W. Berry, *Jayber Crow, 2000,* Counterpoint, Berkely, CA

[181] W. Berry, *Hannah Coulter,* 2004, Counterpoint, Berkely, CA